ADVANCE PRAISE FOR
THE SINGLE PARENT'S MONEY GU...

"The Single Parent's Money Guide will be a classic in n...
equality of women and girls in schools and in the wor...
and supportive of men as well as women who find themselves in a newly-singled life."

FLORENCE D. ANDRÉ
PRESIDENT, ANDRÉ ASSOCIATES, FUND RAISING CONSULTANTS
(FORMELY COUNSELOR TO WOMEN, NEWCOMB COLLEGE)

"As a single parent of four whose youngest child has just graduated from college, I wish I could have had Emily Card's book as a roadmap for my unchartered trip."

BARBARA DAVIS BLUM
CHAIRWOMAN AND CEO, THE ADAMS NATIONAL BANK

"What a wonderful book. It not only deals with the nitty-gritty of finances, but addresses the emotional issues around money that nobody ever talks about in simple, concrete steps so that the problems of raising children alone don't become overwhelming. This book is must reading and will make a great gift to the single or about to become single parent."

LORAINE DESPRES
TELEVISION AND FILM WRITER
BOARD OF DIRECTORS, EL NIDO FAMILY CENTERS

"This book will be a valuable resource for people starting out as single parents."

JUDYE FOY
INTERNATIONAL VICE-PRESIDENT OF COMMUNITY RELATIONS
PARENT'S WITHOUT PARTNERS, INC.

"I would make this book mandatory reading for every single parent. As a single Dad for many years and the founder of a national single parent's organization, I appreciate the practical advice and techniques for all stages of single parenting. From the separation to putting the children through college to a remarriage, The Single Parent's Money Guide covers the gamut. Readers will realize they're not alone and discover options they never thought they had. Very empowering."

EDWARD STANLEY PRICE
FOUNDER & CEO
SINGLE PARENTS ASSOCIATION

"I recommend The Single Parent's Money Guide to anyone going through a divorce or separation. It is a straightforward primer on how to regain control of your life in the face of financial and emotional catastrophe."

PETER M. WALZER
FELLOW OF THE ACADEMY OF MATRIMONIAL LAWYERS

THE
SINGLE PARENT'S MONEY GUIDE

Emily W. Card

with Christie Watts Kelly

Macmillan • USA

ALSO BY EMILY CARD

Staying Solvent: A Comprehensive Guide to Equal Credit for Women
The Ms. Money Book
The Consumer Reports Money Book (co-author)

BY EMILY CARD AND ADAM MILLER

Business Capital for Women
Managing Your Inheritance (forthcoming, 1996)

ISBN: 0-0286-1119-5

Library of Congress Cataloging Card Number: 96-068553

98 97 96   6 5 4 3 2 1

Interpretation of the printing code: the rightmost number of the first series of numbers is the year of the book's printing; the rightmost number of the second series of numbers is the number of the book's printing. For example, a printing code of 96-1 shows that the first printing occurred in 1996.

Printed in the United States of America

Book design by Pixel Press

To Rose Ann Elizabeth Kinard
Carmichael, 1865–1953.
Matriarch and single mother
of nine for almost fifty years.

To Waldo Carmichael Card
Brosveen. You are my
wonderful son who taught me
how to be a single parent.
—Emily

To Mary Barbour Reed,
1955–1992. As a single mother
you were an inspiration. As a
friend you are dearly missed.
—Christie

Acknowledgments

From the accountant who shared his angst about the court systems to the waitress who served us her "tips for a friendly divorce" along with the salads we ordered, all of the single parents we spoke with made a special contribution to this book. We thank them.

In addition, there were a few who stood out as supportive and helpful with this project. Our editor, Debra Wishik Englander at Macmillan Consumer Information Group, was a joy to work with. Agent Denise Marcil brought the project to us and it proved personally and professionally productive. Our family law experts, attorneys R. Miles Mason of Memphis, Tennessee, and Susan Weiss of Santa Monica, California, offered a wealth of information as well as Stuart Raffel, President, and Paul Polapink, Chief Actuary, Price, Raffel, & Browne Administrators, Inc. of Century City, California. And many government officials provided data.

Emily would especially like to thank Broadway Gymnastic School owners Mary and Michael Cates, head coach Henri Vanyetsian and coaches Heinz Schulmeister, Stefan Furst, Hugo Montes, and Darryl Thompson, who have been a second family to my son Waldo. Thanks to David Bryan, Paul and Mary Ann Cummins, and the New Roads School faculty and staff Chris Elder, Marcie Gilbert, Tahira Palmer, Leah Taylor, and Reba Thomas, whose combined commitment to educational diversity and fun has given Waldo a new outlook on school life. Thanks also to Roosevelt Elementary School principal Jerry Harris and to teachers Christie Savage, Angie Snow, Marilyn Hanson, and Ann Whitley for seeing Waldo through grades 1-5 and the First United Methodist of Santa Monica Pre-School for giving him a fine start. Gratitude to Judy Savage for her work for Waldo. Dora Gallardo, Felix Schmitt, and George Solorzano all deserve big hugs for keeping us going at various points during the transition. I want to acknowledge how much my parents, Ray D. Watts and the late Anne Dempsey Watts taught me about parenting and family life. My siblings have contributed as well: sister Janie Spataro, a model mom and source of information; sister Judy Watts, a devoted working mohter who constantly motivates her children to do their best; and brother Dean Watts, a true family man who gives his children the gift of adventure and the space to be individuals. Even though our marriage did not work out, I appreciate all that Kent Brosveen did as a parent when we were together and his acceptance of my need to tell my side of our story. He plans to answer with a song. Mary and Alt Brosveen also are wonderfull grandparents to Waldo. Finally, I owe a lasting debt of gratitude to my co-author on two other books, Adam L. Miller, who constantly encouraged me to shift more of my attention to Waldo.

Christie would like to especially thank Emily Card and Debra Wishik Englander for making my dream of writing a book come true. As an educator, I realize that it wouldn't have been possible without early contributions from my parents, Dean and Gail Watts, who read aloud to me each day as well as the many teachers that touched my life and gave me the skills I needed to excel. My siblings, Tripp, Heather, and Jennifer Watts, have each provided valuable insights as true lifelong friends. After interviewing so many single parents, I have a renewed sense of appreciation for my husband, Shawn, an all-around great guy, and daughter, Arabella, whose hugs and kisses provide a generous reward at the end of a hard day. I couldn't have done it without the excellent childcare provided by grandmother Paulette Goad Kelly, caring baby-sitter Nell Jett, and the wonderful teachers at Christ United Methodist Church. My dear friend and sister-in-law Sissy Kelly Davis, a single parent, offered baby-sitting and moral. Sister-in-law Jeanette Mayo was a model working mom.

Others that helped along the way and paved the way to a smoother journey: The Arlington Hotel in Hot Springs, Arkansas, and Chateau Elan in Atlanta, Georgia, provided inspiring locations for writing retreats, ITT Sheraton Towers served as our New York "home base;" efficient typist Vicki Caudle never complained when we "needed it yesterday;" and consultant Barry Spencer at East Memphis Kinko's made the final marathon more bearable.

Finally, we want to thank all of our unnamed family and friends who proved patient and understanding when the book seemed to overtake our lives.

About the Authors

Single parent Emily Card is an attorney, author, and lecturer who resides in Santa Monica, California. Her work has taken her all around the country, giving her the opportunity to meet other single parents who are looking for a better way.

Christie Watts Kelly is a Memphis, Tennessee-based writer and mother. She drew upon her experience as a teacher and the advice of her many single parent friends for her inspiration on single parenting with an emphasis on the child's perspective.

Although this book was written by two people, it is told from Emily Card's point of view. When possible we have written in a genderless language. Our examples are composites based on Emily's work as a financial consultant and lawyer as well as the informal survey and interviews with single parents from around the country.

We based the information in the book on our findings from these single parents and hope you'll benefit from what you read. Look back from time to time and see how your financial priorities change as your children grow.

The authors welcome your comments and questions about how future editions of this book could better meet your needs.

Write us at:
Parents
P.O. Box 3725
Santa Monica, CA 90403

http:// www.womenmoney.com
ownmoney@aol.com
parents@womenmo.com

Contents

PART THREE:
THE FUTURE 137

Preface

Single parents have the hardest job on earth. Even presidents have cooks, chauffeurs, valets, secretaries, aides, and yes, wives to help them. Single parents have only themselves and their children. All parents have familial, financial, and legal issues with which to contend. But when you're in charge of your own family, the feeling that "the buck stops here" is overwhelming. If you have the flu, if you become disabled, if your mother dies, you must still be on duty for your little ones.

Just this morning, my eleven-year old son, Waldo, burst into tears as I drove him to school. He absolutely, positively could not carry in his homework. He wasn't satisfied with his work, and he wasn't going to school. I struck a deal. If he would go to the attendance office to get his readmission pass, I would carry his homework to the teacher.

When presented with my son's work, the teacher looked alarmed. "He's supposed to have a packet, including the prior drafts. He should have a colored map. Is this all he wrote for his story? Where's his interview?"

Haltingly, I explained Waldo had done the best he could—and fled from the school just as his little shining face came around the corner.

I felt like a complete flop. Here I am with a Ph.D. and a law degree, and we're failing sixth grade!

Over coffee, a close friend suggested seeing a shrink, changing schools, and demanding more help from the school. Her final offering sent me reeling: "Have you ever considered sending him to his father?"

I spent the next hour or so running errands, trying to regain my equilibrium. Could we move to a smaller city? Could I afford private school? Where did I go wrong, so that sixth grade had become a monumental challenge?

Later I ran into another single mom having her own set of school concerns. Her daughter had just switched from a "bilingual" school to one with instruction in English only. Dora said she was on the phone nearly every day with the school counselor trying to overcome Vanessa's problems. Although I felt sorry for them, I also felt better knowing I wasn't alone. I had found a sympathetic ear—not by appointment, not from an official, but from someone who was sharing a similar experience.

Finding such support on the spot proves rare. The crux of the matter? Single parents have no one to share with. No matter how we try to build a network, daily support is hard to find. We're on our own.

You're probably thinking, "Sure, I feel that way too, but what does it have to do with my money?" Finances do not occur in a vacuum. My goal is to place the many tasks single parents face in the context of money and the legal decisions that result from our status.

My own story will shed some light on how I came to write this book. Even though I had been a financial columnist for a major women's magazine and had written three books on money, when I became a single parent, I was totally unprepared. The details of my divorce sound as dreary as the next person's, so I tell my friends that my husband left because I didn't like my birthday present. Let's just say the separation was sudden, though in retrospect, not surprising.

In my household, I was the main breadwinner while my husband spent more time parenting. My immediate reaction was to pretend that nothing had changed, especially with my parenting. I hired replacements to do the driving and to help with homework. Lessons continued, tutoring was added, and life continued for a year as if the adjustments were just temporary. The ex wasn't gone; he was just "out of town."

When tax time came, I woke up to financial reality. Instead of the $5,000 dependent care deduction allowed by Uncle Sam, the tab for keeping Waldo's life the same ran $21,000.

Putting my head in the sand was not only expensive, but also stressful. By continuing to run my law office at full tilt, complete with evening meetings and weekend conferences, I was running myself ragged. Not wanting my son to feel deprived, I juggled more parenting time as well. I landed in the hospital by Christmas, and my aloneness hit me hard. With no one else to turn to, I had to leave Waldo with a housekeeper while I struggled to recover from my physical ailments.

Such experiences drove home the realization that now was the time for far-reaching adjustments. First, I scaled back my law practice to a manageable size, keeping only the clients who didn't bring a heavy dose of stress. Then, I began to pare my time working in the office down to during school hours only. I still had to have help with the driving, because my son is an athlete. A wonderful mother volunteered to drive my son three days a week for a year. I realized that even in our urban community, parents would actually help one another. For me, finding help signaled a turning point.

My next adaptation was to shift my law practice, so I could work more from home and return to writing, which allows a more flexible schedule. Now I am able to be at home in the afternoon when Waldo returns; on driving days, I do the driving myself.

Perhaps because I have made so many adjustments to be a "good enough" parent, mornings such as today hit me hard. But I know that today was just one of those mornings that I have to survive.

These few pages have been hard to write. If my editor had asked me to do a book on almost any other topic, I could have distanced myself a bit. But therapeutic as the exercise is, writing this book means I have to address issues that would be easier to just sweep under the rug. How many people want to admit that they've failed in a marriage and are challenged as parents?

I hope the shared experience will demonstrate to other single parents that a better job or more money aren't the only issues to resolve and that we can't blame all our troubles on money. If, like me, you're a career-minded single parent, I hope you can give yourself permission, as I did, to slow down and enjoy these precious few years. Finally, I hope that you, like me, will come to terms with this most difficult of challenges, being the primary (or only) adult responsible for the lives of your children.

When the time came to write this book, I turned to one of the most engaged parents I know, Christie Watts Kelly. I knew that Christie's perspective as an educator, researcher, and writer from a different region of the country would enrich what I had to contribute.

Both of us hope that this book will help you find your path to financial security as a single parent. You probably didn't sign up for the job you have. But as one mother expressed to me while we waited for our cars in a New Orleans parking lot, "You'll never regret a minute of the time you spend with your child."

P.S. I did change Waldo's school at mid-term, which I considered a drastic step, and he's flourishing in his new school home

Introduction

Today nearly one-third of U.S. families are headed by single parents. We now outnumber the "traditional family model" (two married parents and their children living at home) four to one. Arrangements that seemed unconventional only a generation ago are now the norm. This dramatic restructuring of the family has outpaced society's ability to deal with the changing financial and legal needs of single parents.

Further challenging our stereotypes are the substantial numbers of single fathers in our ranks. In 1994, an estimated 1.6 million single-parent families were headed by men. That same year saw 9.9 million single mothers, still a vast majority. However, this book is for all single-parent families—whether headed by men or women—recognizing that each family faces unique challenges and circumstances, yet all have much in common.

We can't wrap ourselves in statistics at night and be comforted because we're together in our aloneness. But by understanding the numbers, we place ourselves in perspective.

WHY SINGLE PARENTS NEED THIS BOOK

Although single parenting is on the rise, alimony and child support are on the decline—$5 billion in back child support is owed in California alone. The same reasons that made it more possible for women to leave intolerable marriages now contribute to a court and societal point of view that women can and should take care of themselves and their children. Since men generally earn more, they are far more likely to be able to take care of themselves and their children as single parents. But both men and women face financial challenges, from dealing with child care to the prospect of coping with blended families should they remarry.

Now more than ever, women earn enough money to support themselves and their families. While many conservatives look on this change as ungluing the family, in fact, before economic independence, women often found themselves and their children in abusive, cruel

SINGLE PARENTS ARE HERE TO STAY

Of the 11.4 million single-parent families in 1994:

MARITAL STATUS

Approximately 38 percent were divorced, 38 percent were never married, 20 percent were separated, and 5 percent were widowed.

LIVING QUARTERS

Nine million maintained their own households, 1.8 million lived with relatives, and 650,000 shared quarters with unrelated families.

GENDER

86 percent were women and 14 percent were men.

RACIAL AND ETHNIC ORIGINS

7.3 million were white (representing 25 percent of all white families), 3.6 million were black (representing about 67 percent of all black families), and about 1.6 million were Hispanic. Data is not available for other racial or ethnic groups.

Source: United States Census Bureau Household and Family Characteristics, March 1994. Figures based on family groups of a single parent with one or more of their children under 18 living in the same residence.

circumstances. Even in physically safe families, women tolerated traumatic or even discordant lives because they had no economic routes out. Men, too, have been freed from staying in marriages that don't work.

As the stigma of divorce has lessened and state divorce laws have changed to reflect changing social mores, the outmoded caricature of the ex-wife with big alimony or the ex-husband who is left childless has died. Now, we see families struggling to keep their thread even when the marriage doesn't last. We also see joint custody, blended families, and families with same-sex parents.

Moreover, it's a commonplace saying that "there's no training for parenthood." Yet cultural imagery provides us guidance, and many of today's single parents grew up in two-parent homes. In 1970, there were only 3.8 million single parents compared with 1994's 11.4 million. The U. S. Census Bureau projects a steady growth in the number of single parents of about 3 percent per year. This trend means that we were likely to have been raised by a two-family model, but our children will be more likely to be raised by single parents. When we look to our own experience as guidance, we are ignoring our own present needs. If we find a way to overcome this obstacle, we will do our children a favor. They will learn that it's possible to survive and flourish in a variety of situations.

Single parents don't have financial role models. The rapid changes in the demographic world, with sitcoms to match, haven't been paired with corresponding shifts in our understanding about how to handle the day-to-day details of finances, legal issues, and planning for the future. While many sitcom characters complain about money troubles, few solutions appear. Solutions don't provide laughs; problems do.

Advertisements contain more about financial planning for college than the shows they sponsor. When was the last time you saw a serious discussion in an entertainment-oriented show that dealt with what steps to take if your child was college bound in five years? On TV, the adolescents focus on sex drives, not college preparations.

Our cultural icons are more akin to *Father Knows Best* or even *Roseanne* than to *Grace Under Fire,* a TV show featuring a single mother struggling to make it on her own. In one of the oddities of TV programming, single fathers fare a bit better. A string of TV fathers have kept watch over mixed broods for several decades. From *Bonanza* to *The Nanny,* fathers are at least shown in command rather than struggling to keep afloat. In the magical world of television, the single father is more likely to have a butler than bills to pay. Single-father readers of this book know better.

It's not easy challenging the cultural stereotype that all single fathers are well-heeled widowers. In addition to fighting the usual battles, because they are still relatively rare, single fathers don't have as many built-in supports as single mothers do. For example, most of the people attending child-oriented functions, such as PTA meetings, tend to be women. A newly single dad may find himself feeling out of place and lacking peer support.

Because money is more private than sex in our society, examples of how other single parents cope are hard to find. To gain the information and insights to manage your money, you need help from other places, such as this book. Or as my son learned in tonight's homework assignment, from "secondary" rather than "primary" sources. Unless you have had the chance to study the pocketbooks of other single parents, as we have, you won't find the primary sources easy to come by.

SINGLE PARENT'S CHECKLIST

To shift your financial life in more productive directions, you need to understand and be able to do the following:

- ☑ Budget your money and time.
- ☑ Control your cash and credit.
- ☑ Balance your needs with your child's needs.
- ☑ Plan for both your future and your child's future.
- ☑ Invest both your money and your child's money.

These tasks are daunting to any parent—after all, this checklist could as easily describe a parent with a mate. As a single parent, you have added challenges. You must

- ☑ Do it alone.
- ☑ Do it without backup.
- ☑ Do it and preserve childhood, resisting the temptation to draw your children into adult roles.
- ☑ Do it despite criticism from the noncustodial parent, in-laws, sisters, and yes, even yourself.

These checklists provide us with guidelines for what we must do, but anyone who thinks they'll find magical answers hasn't been there. Lifestyle choices must be altered; compromises made. Change doesn't happen overnight. In this book, I focus on concrete, achievable steps that each parent can take one at a time to feel a daily sense of accomplishment while preparing for the next step.

CHANGING PERSPECTIVES

Shifts in thinking must occur inside us as well as in society. In a 1948 speech, Mahatma Gandhi gave us a key to defining our single-parent attitudes in his description of a business customer:

> A customer is the most important visitor on our premises. He is not dependent on us, we are dependent on him. He is not an interruption of our work, he is the purpose of it. He is not an outsider on our business, he is a part of it. We are not doing him a favor by serving him. He is doing us a favor by giving us an opportunity to do so.

Likewise, when we see our children as a distraction from our lives, we will struggle against our role as single parents, just as the businessperson going over the cash receipts will miss the next sale to the customer at the counter.

How often do we think, "If only I weren't a single parent, I could go to the symphony," or "If only I could meet someone new, but I don't have time to date," or "My child keeps me so busy I don't have time for my friends." These thoughts are valid, but they also place the child in the role of interrupter—of our quiet moment, of our business day, of our adult lives.

We can turn around our perspective while still acknowledging our own needs. In later chapters, we'll offer tips on taking care of yourself. However, a very real part of taking care of ourselves is to accept who and what we are now. Now we are single parents. Maybe our days of dancing until 3:00 A.M. have been replaced by the opportunity to dance at 3:00 P.M. with our little ones. *Our children are not an interruption of our work. They are the purpose of it.*

Accepting my role as a single parent, bending with it instead of fighting against it, was my first step toward refocusing my life personally, professionally, and financially. I hope this perspective will help you, too.

PART ONE

Where Am I and Where Do I Want to Be?

CHAPTER 1

Assessing Your Unique Situation

Many single parents are on the financial, emotional, and legal edge, postponing key tasks because they can't seem to cope with today's breakfast, tonight's homework, or tomorrow's deadline. The routes to single parenthood may vary from separation, divorce, or death of the other parent to less conventional roads such as artificial insemination, adoption, or the choice to remain unwed. Other important variables include the number of children, accustomed standard of living, and employment status. Each variable creates additional issues to consider as you place yourself among the 11.4 million parents for whom this book was written.

VARIABLES THAT AFFECT YOU

Your situation determines your needs and outlook. Let's take a look at four key elements that can influence your actions and perceptions. These include the *timing* of your single status, the *choice* you had in the situation, the *difficulty* of your divorce or separation, and the available *finances* after the event.

Timing

It's often said, "timing is everything." In assessing your situation, *timing* plays two important roles. First, consider the timing of your single status.

SINGLE PARENT CONTINUUM
Separated ➡ In a Messy Divorce ➡ Just Divorced ➡ Widow/er ➡ Several Years ➡ Never Married

Where do you fall on the "single-parent continuum"? The answer to that question will, in turn, determine the timing of critical financial decisions.

A newly widowed mother of four with good insurance has a different set of challenges from a man fighting for custody of his two young daughters. Yet each group's distinct entry pattern to solo parenthood should lead to a single financial road, one that involves gaining control and exercising caution.

If you're like most people, you're reading this book because you're in pain. Perhaps you've just been separated, and you're grasping at straws—anything to get your feet on the ground. Or you've been alone awhile, but you stalled the process of altering your life, as I did, to fit your new circumstances. If you didn't allow time, you'll need to go back and pick up the threads, including mourning if necessary.

Even if the absent partner is still living, you need to allow yourself time to mourn the end of your relationship while avoiding rash decisions. Particularly about finances, decisions that you make hastily can haunt you for years. For example, if a newly separated mother copies her mate and buys her own midlife-crisis red convertible, she may be using money that would have been better dedicated to retirement savings. If she understood how timing affects her choices, she might have decided she could live with a new paint job on her old car while treating herself to a less expensive splurge.

Follow these guidelines to allow yourself the time that you need:

- **Be conservative with your money.** Go into a "holding pattern." Maintain your monthly bills, and don't spend extravagantly.

- **Educate yourself.** Read this book, go to support groups or seminars, find a mentor.

- **Invest in yourself.** Return to school for a higher earning potential, repair your psyche by seeking professional help, and keep yourself healthy.

- **Avoid get-rich-quick schemes.** It's okay to play the lottery occasionally, but avoid large lump-sum investments. Seek the advice of a trusted lawyer before making major financial decisions.

Choice

While time may heal all wounds, when we don't have a *choice* in our status, we can be left bitter. You know the story. The husband runs off with a younger woman. The wife leaves her workaholic husband for a ski bum. A dearly beloved spouse dies in a diving accident. All these scenarios leave us wishing we could turn back the clock. We think through the scenes, replaying them with different endings. These are the "what ifs?" that govern our emotional responses.

Or perhaps you had a choice in the matter, but now you're feeling overwhelmed in the face of your challenges. Look back to the reasons you first decided to become a single parent, and feel empowered by having made this bold decision.

Despite the alchemists' and space travelers' attempts, no one has yet discovered a way to turn back time. So we are left with our choices—or lack of them. Emotionally and financially, we must avoid feeling stuck or helpless and learn to move on to future choices with a fresh outlook.

Difficulty

No matter how lovely the orange blossoms and how happy the newlyweds, some divorces become more bitter and acrimonious than others. No one can predict which couple will turn into the "War of the Roses." Patterns that developed during the marriage or relationship can serve as clues. Couples with a history of unfair fighting may become "pit bulls" in the divorce courts. Other times, both spouses are relieved to bring this chapter to a close, and they move smoothly through the transition.

Whenever children are involved—and we're assuming they are or were because this book is for single parents—their presence ups the ante.

Even the most mellow financial settlements turn topsy-turvy when it comes to arranging for the children. Worse yet, the looming threat of fighting over custody often leads to making difficult financial compromises. When faced with a "your-money-or-your-children" choice, many parents sacrifice future financial security for current custody.

The hardest thing about a divorce is that you cannot control the actions of the other spouse. (If you could, you wouldn't be divorcing, would you?) Being dependent on your spouse's often seemingly irrational reactions intensifies your own emotional responses.

ACCEPTANCE EXERCISE

When anyone said she was old, my mother always replied: "Consider the alternative."
If you have difficulty accepting your single status, think about the alternatives.
I firmly believe that each step we take brings us to exactly where we are, and we are at this position to learn its lesson. If we refuse to learn, we stay stuck.
The only way out is through. Make this your mantra. Move on through.

No easy answers are offered here. The wisest course of action is to take it slow and to remember that most of what you fear may happen never will.

A case in point: One husband demanded 16 weekend visits a year. The wife had to agree to pay for half the airfares to a city 500 miles away. When she balked, a wise friend said, "Even though my husband was a drunk, I wish he'd kept more involved in the children's lives." The couple compromised at 12 visits, and guess what? "Pinning down a schedule when my son can conveniently visit his father has become the challenge," says this mother.

Most of what you fear may happen never will.

Part of dealing with the difficulty and accepting whatever problems are hurled your way is helped by thinking about your own contributions to the split. The Japanese play *Rashomon* illustrates the point best. Each character's story of the same experience is told from a different point of view, and their different versions demonstrate how subjective our perceptions can be. If your "he said, she said" litany grows tiring, turn to making changes in yourself to shape a more palatable life.

Remember, difficulties can rob you of the momentum you need to restore order and change directions. If your finances are to be sound, you need to let go of as much concern with difficulty as you can, and focus on change instead.

Finances

Worrying about money has become a national pastime. From Congress battling the deficit to strapped families ferreting out a living, money has replaced religion as the centerpiece of our national culture. Americans have always been more materialistic than many other cultures. In the past, however, the professions, the arts, the academics, and even the government were respected institutions in which one's mastery wasn't measured in one-dimensional terms. Financial success as measured by the accumulation of money has replaced other forms of measuring accomplishment. The only near rival is celebrity, but this flash point has become so intertwined with being well-off that the public is surprised when the famous aren't rich or the rich don't wish to enjoy fame.

In this milieu, no wonder those of us left holding the center sometimes feel on the financial fringes. While we can imitate riches, using credit cards or vacationing, the grim reality for most single parents is that money is tight—very tight. It's no accident that the standard of living of most women falls 30 percent after divorce, because most children live with their mothers. By contrast with high-profile media stories, few divorcees get lucrative divorce settlements or generous alimony.

In fact, of the 20.6 million ever-divorced or currently separated women in 1990, only 15.5 percent were awarded alimony. That number hasn't shifted significantly since 1978, when the percentage was 14.3 percent. The women most likely to be parents—women under 40—were only half as likely to receive alimony. The truth is, alimony is a myth for most. Stories of men "losing everything" told on country club golf courses are fairy tales. Women who sit in aerobics classes and share stories of deadbeat husbands who gained lifetime security are fabricating fables. The numbers show a different story: Divorce is not enriching.

Custodial fathers, too, experience a drop in lifestyle concomitant with becoming single parents. But the decline slope is less steep, because women earn less and thus have less to contribute to the prior lifestyle. Looking at it another way, the husband's earnings were and will remain higher.

FACT:

The U.S. Census Bureau does not track alimony payments awarded to men.

Even when alimony is awarded, the formulas by which alimony and child support are calculated rarely give the custodial parent more than 40 percent of the prior family income, no matter how many children are involved. And while child support awards are somewhat higher, getting awards and actually collecting them are two different stories. Though the figures are not available for men, in 1990 almost 30 percent of women awarded child support sought government assistance in collecting it.

If you're among the lucky few who receive regular alimony or child support payments, count your blessings but don't count on the money's continuing indefinitely. You must learn to plan and live within a budget based on what you can earn, because statistics suggest that your payments won't continue. If you're among the one-third of all divorcing women receiving property settlements, your number-one financial priority is to hold on to what you've achieved and to protect it.

While these same points apply to the smaller numbers of men in the same position, they're especially important for women because

- Women continue to earn less than men in all fields.

- Women's earning curves flatten out at age 40, while men's continue to rise into their 50s.

- Women live longer and are less likely to be entitled to pensions of their own.

What if you also get a settlement that includes debt or tax obligations? Your challenge is even greater, because you'll need to balance the temporary serenity of paying it all back against the future security of keeping your capital intact. If you can guard your capital from the collectors, you'll have a much better chance of surviving your financial transition.

A friend of mine involved in divorcing a well-known professor telephoned me to say she was just about to give up her home to achieve a less lengthy negotiation. I told her what I'll tell you: "Keep your home. It's your base. Without a home, achieving a secure retirement is very difficult, because rents always rise." Her question was, "But what if I don't want to live there anymore?" My response: "If at all possible, rent it. Your house can provide a steady income stream."

Write this note and post it where you negotiate your divorce or plan your finances: *Keep my home.*

Even if you're very strapped for cash, you should think long and hard before selling your home. It will be very difficult for you to amass that much capital again as a single parent. If your spouse wants to divide the equity in the house, try to negotiate so that you can keep it until your children have graduated from high school.

Of course, I recognize that not all single parents will have a home to keep. As we look at specific strategies for each situation, we'll discuss different options for different lifestyles and financial positions. Whether it's a home, valuable art, jewelry, or a savings bond, the rule remains: Keep it.

We've looked at the variables of timing, choice, difficulty, and finances as key points that make each of our stories different. Let's return to issues that concern all single parents.

UNIVERSAL ISSUES

All single parents, almost without exception, concern themselves with a number of personal questions. These include lack of adult companionship; time for oneself; the fear of growing old alone after devoting years to raising children; and numerous other fears.

In addition, the single parent has become a political football, blamed on the one hand for poverty, crime, and the decline of family values; on the other, for raising children that will be inferior in any number of ways, from school performance to career advancement. Studies show a correlation between divorce and problems with children, yet little is done in schools, churches, or politics to support this brave breed who daily defy the odds and try to raise their children properly despite prejudices and misunderstandings.

Gestalt (gə-shtält') A unified whole.

If the eye sees U, the mind thinks O. If we see our family as complete, we don't ask our mind to make the extra step, but ourselves to accept that we are whole.

My O family.

Let me share one pet peeve that illustrates how insensitive schools can be. When my son enrolled in his new public middle school, the paperwork featured space for both parents with a box to check next to the custodial parent. Naturally, the father was listed first, so despite my indication on the card that the child was in my custody, every mailed notice from the school arrives addressed to "Parent of Waldo Card" followed by my husband's name. Despite my efforts to correct the mailing label, it's clear that for three years the "parent" will continue to be the absentee parent. It's a cruel little reminder, usually on a bad day, that someone is missing from our family.

While this book is not meant to be a pop-psychology manifesto, I recognize that these personal, nonfinancial concerns affect your financial well-being. Emotional ups and downs contribute to financial ups and downs and vice versa. For example, if I received my school's notice on the same day as an unexpectedly large long-distance phone bill, I might find myself focusing on my missing spouse instead of the immediate issue of cutting long-distance phone charges. Psychology comes into play with money, whether or not we want it to.

My mission is to give you the best possible guidance that will result in a healthy financial life shored up by firm legal underpinnings. While psychological adjustment is secondary to our main purpose, to achieve those underpinnings, you must learn to change nonfinancial areas along the following lines:

1. Change your thinking.

2. Develop new habits.

3. Exercise your choices.

Change Your Thinking

Waldo sometimes says, "I wish we had a family." My response is, "We are a family." If you continue to think of yourself and your child as missing something rather than as a complete family, you'll continue to make decisions as if the missing white knight will return. It's easier to continue to avoid the reality that you and your family have changed.

Russian studies have shown that when people think often about a task, they will later remember it as if they had finished it. Synapses (connecting cells) in the brain will "complete the memory circuit," creating a false memory that seems true.

If you think of your family as missing a piece, your mind will create a false perception to support those thoughts. Feeling like a "temporary" or incomplete family prevents us from seeing our financial needs clearly. If we assume that someone else will provide retirement security or take care of us in a medical emergency, we won't solve these issues for ourselves.

Develop New Habits

When you go to the supermarket, how often do you study each item you buy? Most of us dash through the market, picking up tried-and-true brands. If we become label detectives, it's usually at the start of a new diet. Otherwise, it's easier and simpler to continue selecting products we know work for us. Our children have their favorites; we have ours.

With financial decisions, we often act the same way. For example, if you take for granted that Saturday night means going out, you probably don't stop to add the cost of your movie and popcorn or the entry fee to a local club. Or if you grew up around a type of business where you didn't have to pay full price, you probably tend to discount the money you spend on the formerly discounted items. My father owned a drugstore, so I have a hard time counting money in a drugstore as "real." Likewise, my sister's husband's family owned a deli. To this day, when he goes to the market, Tony buys large packages and giant bunches of fruit even if only for himself. These examples illustrate the power of financial habits.

> **Our habits control us. If we change our habits, then good habits will control us.**
> —GYMNASTICS COACH

You probably have many financial habits that are so ingrained you never think twice about them. From using an expensive dry cleaner to making long-distance calls during peak hours, habits are hard to break. If we had to think through each step of every day, we'd be exhausted; therefore, we don't want to rid ourselves of habits, but to create new ones.

Setting up new habits takes time and patience. If you attempt to correct all your financial misdemeanors at once, you'll defeat yourself before you start. Begin gradually. Pick one or two easy items and work on those. For example, if you buy a newspaper every morning from a vending machine, order home delivery. It's cheaper and, depending on your line of work, might be deductible as a business expense on your income taxes. Or if you always buy soda when you eat out, try drinking water for a month. Every time you save a dollar or two, put the money in a special place—such as your car ashtray—and use it for a special treat.

Exercise Your Choices

In yoga class last Saturday, the teacher talked about the choices we have over our lives as the students continued their breathing and postures. Just as I was feeling that anything was possible, a woman in the corner of the room cried out: "We have no choices. If you don't do what they want, they'll kill you." A shudder ran through the room, not a mile from where the Nicole Brown-Simpson and Ronald Goldman murders had occurred.

Women often feel they don't have choices because in the past, men's wills have been exercised through physical power. Even if that power only resides in the subconscious as a suggestion, women speak of empowerment often because they have so long been without it. When suddenly our lives change and we can make our own choices, we are sometimes overwhelmed by the possibilities. Without choices, it's easier for us to assume the presence of an "other" looking over our shoulder, even when there's no one there but our own fear.

Likewise, in the past, men's lives were often dictated by the assumptions of being the breadwinner for a family, and careers and life choices were made accordingly. Even for men unsuited to family leadership, before the women's movement helped shift perspectives, the "man of the house" was stuck with the role, like it or not. Currently, role-modeling for men as single parents is limited. Men who have chosen this role or had it thrust upon them, like their female counterparts, must look at new ways to make choices, but often without as much guidance from those who've "been there."

The essence of financial change lies in making new financial choices. Learning to make new choices about what we have can transform our financial lives. Let's look at the choices you've been making.

FINANCIAL FITNESS QUIZ

This brief checklist is only a beginning. Don't worry if you must answer no to most questions. By the end of the book, you'll be answering yes or have strategies in place to achieve them.

FINANCIAL FITNESS:
WHERE DO YOU STAND AND WHERE DO YOU WANT TO BE?

	Now	*Date to Do*
1. Do you have a written budget?	_____	_____
2. Are your credit cards under control?	_____	_____
3. Do you know where to find your property?	_____	_____
4. Do you have a list of all your bank accounts in one place?	_____	_____
5. Are your savings enough to see you through three months?	_____	_____
6. Do you have a disability insurance policy? How much? Where is the policy kept?	_____	_____
7. Do you have a life insurance policy? How much? Where is it?	_____	_____
8. Do you have an IRA, KEOGH, 401(k), or pension?	_____	_____

9. Is your will written? _____ _____

10. Does your will contain guardianship provisions for your child? _____ _____

11. Have you made investments on your own? _____ _____

12. Do you have advisors you can trust? _____ _____

13. Do you have a health insurance policy for the entire family? _____ _____

14. Have you paid your student loans? _____ _____

15. Are your taxes filed up to date? _____ _____

RESOURCES

Bob Deits. *Life After Loss: A Personal Guide to Dealing with Death, Divorce, Job Change and Relocation.* Tucson, Ariz.: Fisher Books, 1992.

Terry Hershey. *Beginning Again.* Nashville: T. Nelson, 1986.

Gerald Jampolsky. *Love is Letting Go of Fear.* Millbrae, Calif.: Celestial Arts, 1979.

Susan Jeffers. *Feel the Fear and Do it Anyway.* San Diego: Harcourt/Brace Jovanovich, 1987.

Hal and Susan Larson. *A Lifeline for Anyone Who has Lost a Love.* San Francisco: Halo books, 1993.

Scott M. Peck. *The Road Less Traveled.* New York: Simon & Schuster, 1978.

Carol Tavris. *Anger: The Misunderstood Emotion.* Rev. ed., New York: Simon & Schuster, 1989.

Abigail Trafford. *Crazy Time: Surviving Divorce.* Rev. ed. New York: HarperPerennial, 1992.

Ellie Wymard. *Men on Divorce: Conversations with Ex-Husbands.* Carson, Calif.: Hay House, 1994.

CHAPTER 2

Timely Goals for Troubling Transitions

Separation and divorce account for the majority of single parents in America. Overwrought and emotionally charged situations can lead to poor financial judgment and instill habits that are fine for survival but will impede future success. Where do you fall on this time line? Are you just stepping into the chasm of a divorce settlement with no "parachute" to protect you? Are you still in shock from your fresh wounds and attempting to keep everything the same at the cost of your future financial security? Or have you been here awhile, hardened to your misery, in a self-created rut?

While this chapter was written for those who are going (or have gone) through a divorce, others may find parts of themselves in these pages. In "About-to-Be's" and "Newly-D's," you'll find that you're going through a grieving process that is similar to that of a widowed single parent. "Seasoned Singles" is about hope. It can teach us all about reaching inside and finding that dream we've lost in our day-to-day struggle.

> **67% of single parent households are due to marital separation and divorce.**
> —UNITED STATES CENSUS BUREAU, 1990

ABOUT-TO-BE'S (WHEN DIVORCE IS ON THE HORIZON)

With your impending separation or divorce, you're faced with a monumental challenge: fear of the unknown. Outwardly, you're dealing with a severing of a bond that you would have once believed unbreakable. Inwardly, you may feel paralyzed, angry, afraid, or even calm, as if nothing is really happening.

If any of those feelings seem familiar to you, you're not alone. But for your own and your children's best interests, you must reach somewhere inside and find the strength and clarity to go on. Clarity is the key at this crux, when your actions and decisions will affect your future well-being. In high school geometry we learned that the shortest route between point A and point B is a straight line. Are you walking a straight line in your divorce process? Or are you taking a more circuitous route out of ambivalence about your relationship? When faced with a seemingly insurmountable task, we instinctively hedge; hoping it will go away. Your challenge: coming to terms with your pending divorce and taking the straightest line that you can muster to get through it. Your reality: the unknown. Your mantra: a line from an old Girl Scout song, "Can't go under it, can't go around it, I'll have to go through it."

Going Straight Through

What's mine, yours, ours… everything's so confusing at this time! But it's up to you to rise above this confusion with some foresight and clarity about what you really need. Family practice lawyer R. Miles Mason recommends the following three key questions as a starting point:

1. Have the divorce papers actually been filed? I'm not here to help you decide if your marriage can be salvaged. With the help of your most trusted friends and advisors, only you can answer that question. But remember, a divorce is a lawsuit. There are two procedural advantages to the party that files first (known as the plaintiff). First, the plaintiff controls the progress of the case. Second, if it actually goes to trial the plaintiff goes first and gets to lay out the facts of the case to the judge. A good lawyer can present the facts to your benefit.

2. Have I chosen my own divorce lawyer? Trying to save money by sharing a lawyer with your spouse may only cost you more (and, most important, your children more) down the road. Horror stories abound, as many single parents have learned the hard way, finding out the loopholes in their Marital Dissolution Agreements (settlements) that cost them child support, insurance benefits, or even custody of the children.

Don't be afraid to talk to more than one lawyer, considering fee arrangements in detail and noting what percentage of the lawyer's practice is in divorce law. For more specific characteristics to look for, consult *Divorcing* by Melvin Belli.

Have your own lawyer draft the Marital Dissolution Agreement if at all possible. If your spouse has already presented you with one, you should have your lawyer go over it with a fine-tooth comb. Common pitfalls and loopholes will be discussed in the box that follows.

DRIVING A HARD BARGAIN

Daniele Reese was stunned when her husband returned home from a routine business trip and announced that he wanted out. In hindsight, she admits that there were warning signs, but at the time he dropped the bomb, she felt that they were happily married and sharing in the joy of their newborn son. Although filled with pain and confusion, she acted quickly and decisively by following her lawyer's advice: Though her husband was the one that wanted out, if she filed the divorce papers, she would be more likely to get the terms she desired. She asked for (and got) the house and all its contents, one of the vehicles, the maximum percentage of child support allowed by the state, and sole custody of the baby. She drove a tough bargain on paper, while he was willing to sign anything to get out. Later, she encouraged the father's involvement by a liberal visitation policy to keep things running smoothly.

3. What is my budget? Determine monthly income and expenses for yourself and your children by creating a basic budget worksheet. Ask your lawyer for one, or turn to Chapter 5 for more on budgeting. Most states have a *Pendente Lite* statute that allows collection of child support, alimony, and even attorney's fees while the divorce is pending. Ask your lawyer whether this is appropriate in your circumstances. In general, "child support payments should begin as soon as possible. If you don't train them now, you can't train them later," Mason warns.

TERMS TO NEGOTIATE: WHAT YOU NEED TO KNOW

Following are some of the terms you'll negotiate in your Marital Dissolution Agreement (MDA). The issues raised here are meant only to help you evaluate your needs. Please consult your own lawyer to determine what provisions are most appropriate (and possible) for your circumstances.

Alimony: Especially in marriages under 10 years duration, courts now favor rehabilitative alimony to give the nonworking spouse a chance to reenter the workforce. The judge will want to see that you've got a plan for college or career training. Alimony awards are generally based on need and obligor's (payer's) ability to pay, although fault is sometimes considered in setting the amount. Reminder: Any income from alimony payments is subject to federal income taxes and is tax deductible for the obligor.

Bankruptcy: Including certain clauses in your MDA can protect you from your ex's potential bankruptcy.

Business Liabilities: If ex owns a sole proprietorship in which marital property (such as vehicles) were donated, sever ties in the same manner as with real estate (see "Real Estate" later in this box).

Child Support: Most states set minimum limits as a percentage of the obligor's income. Don't let feelings of guilt or pity for the obligor prevent you from collecting the full amount required by law or from getting started as soon as possible. If you have a special needs child, include provisions for higher payments and require them to continue past the standard cutoff (typically age 18). For tax purposes, child support is nondeductible for the obligor and nonincludable as income for the recipient.

Custody: Regardless of physical custody, be specific about who has the final say and on what matters. For consistency and safety, the custodial parent should have the decision-making authority. Caution: In some states equally shared physical custody negates the requirement for child support payments. Prevent this outcome by naming a primary custodial parent and standard visitation for the noncustodial parent, keeping in mind that you can always allow more visitation than the minimum requirements.

Credit Cards: Before you cancel and cut up all jointly held credit cards (the balance will remain, but no new charges can be made) try to determine the primary holder of the card especially if you didn't have one in your own name already.

While it's illegal under the Equal Credit Opportunity Act (ECDA) for a creditor to cancel a credit card upon change in marital status, you do have to show creditors how you will repay the balances. Include a provision on the MDA determining how the balances will be paid.

Educational Trusts: If feasible, require the noncustodial parent to deposit part of monthly child support in a trust fund. Find a mutual fund that allows you to invest in small monthly increments such as $50. Have the brokerage house set up an educational trust document for each child that will prevent withdrawal of funds for anything other than educational expenses.

Health Insurance: If you have been covered under your spouse's health insurance policy, federal law requires the coverage to continue for up to 36 months after your divorce. Determine whether you or your spouse will pay for the coverage until you find new insurance. Never let your health insurance lapse under any circumstances (see Chapter 11).

Life Insurance: MDA can require the noncustodial parent to purchase a set amount of life insurance with the children as beneficiaries.

Personal Property: Try to divide everything before the MDA is signed. Otherwise, anything important that you want back should be listed in the MDA.

Property Settlement: Keep in mind that the transfer of property is not taxed at divorce, but the basis is transferred for future calculations on capital gains.

Real Estate: Try to keep your home if at all possible. But, if you don't live in the house, take your name off the mortgage. If the noncustodial parent keeps the house, your MDA can require that the spouse make "good faith efforts" to refinance, removing your name from the mortgage loan. If that doesn't take place, include a provision forcing the sale of the house, so that you can divide the proceeds and be free of any future obligations.

Retirement Plans: Although these can be the largest asset in a divorce, they are often overlooked. If your spouse has a significant amount of money in one, consult your lawyer about the best way to handle it. You may also contact the Pension Rights Center, (see Chapter resources).

Will: If there is a likelihood that the noncustodial parent will remarry and have another family, require that the spouse leave 30 percent to 50 percent of the estate to the children from your union (see Chapter 14).

Negotiating for the Support You Need

You must enter the divorce settlement process knowing the property settlement you want: how much alimony and child support. What do you need from the missing parent? What can you provide yourself? Ask yourself, do I have a job? If yes, do I earn enough to support my family without child support? Will it be enough if I get the house? If no, do I have marketable skills? Should I ask for alimony (spousal support) to tide me over until I get those career skills?

Know what you need, what you want, and what you're willing to negotiate on. Know what you're asking for and why. Be careful what you ask for, remembering the adage that "you might just get what you ask for." Think of a divorce settlement like an investment portfolio. Don't put your eggs in one basket because you don't know what might happen to the basket. For example, if you put all your "eggs" in the child support or alimony "basket" rather than the property settlement "basket," you'll be up the creek without a basket if your former spouse gets laid off.

NEWLY-D'S (FOR THE RECENTLY DIVORCED)

It's over. Good or bad, you've got your settlement. Or you're stuck in the limbo of a long separation, waiting for the divorce to be final. Either way, you're on your own. Sometimes circumstances will drive this point ever so poignantly home; for example, when you're setting one less place at the dinner table, or you don't even have a dinner table because your ex took it. Don't put your life on hold any longer. Life must go on. Your challenge: Learning to live *without* the income from your settlement, because you're the only one you can really count on. Your reality: Coping with the day-to-day existence with no time to worry about the future. Your mantra: I will survive.

You must believe that you will not only survive, but also flourish under your evolving conditions. You may, however, feel overwhelmed by your new situation. Realize that the waves of change are already washing over you. Let yourself ride with the waves rather than be overcome by them. For example, if you're operating on a lower than accustomed to income, you'll have to downsize sooner or later. Instead of waiting for a credit crisis, why not downsize now? Being forced to do it later would be disheartening and increase your sense of loss. But choosing to do it now can be empowering, especially if you form clear goals to remind you that your present sacrifices are ultimately worthwhile.

On the other hand, don't make your goals so general and idealistic that there's no connection with your daily life. While you'll want some big goals to set your compass by, you must rely on reaching smaller ones to keep up your spirits and to focus clearly.

Your financial life follows a parallel course to your emotional healing. The first year should be a time of adjustment, of shoring up resources, and of taking stock. The flux of emotions you're experiencing will affect everyday spending habits and make it difficult to even think about long-term decisions. In the first weeks and months, you'll be letting go of old systems and setting up your own routines for paying bills, making deposits, and ensuring your daily financial survival. Only after some normalcy has returned should you consider any far-reaching financial moves such as liquidating assets, making lump-sum investments, or making large purchases such as a house or car.

SMALL SUCCESSES; BIG REWARDS

If you're reading this book during the first year of your separation or divorce, you may feel overwhelmed by all that it asks of you. One single mother we interviewed said, "How can I think about trying to hire a housekeeper when I don't even know if I can afford to buy a can of Lysol!" Likewise, planning for college and retirement, making a will, and comparing insurance policies seem like impossible tasks when you can't even seem to find the time to balance your checkbook. So start small. Below are some personal financial milestones most people encounter in the first year. Remember that each small success takes you one step closer to your post-divorce financial goals.

First Days:
Secure your share of cash and credit assets.

1. Withdraw one-half of all jointly held checking and savings accounts.

2. Open new checking and savings accounts in your name.

3. Protect the credit you now hold.

First Weeks:
Make sure life insurance benefits go to your child, not your ex.

1. Call or write your life insurance company indicating your decision for changing your beneficiary.

2. Name your children as your beneficiaries. If they are minors leave the benefits to a guardian or trustee until they come of age (for example you can name your bank as trustee).

Remove your ex as a beneficiary of your will.

1. Call your lawyer and change your beneficiary to someone more appropriate, such as your children.

2. Make sure you sign and date your will and specify that it replaces all previous wills.

3. See Chapter 14 for ideas on where to store your documents.

Name a financial guardian for your children.

Cancel your ex's power of attorney, if one has ever existed.

First Months:
Get rid of those pesky (and sometimes depressing) reminders.

If your divorce settlement left you with the house, chances are that bills from the telephone company, utilities, and even the exterminator might still be in your spouse's name. The hassles of changing it will depend on the extent of your local bureaucracy.

Many women choose to keep their married names so they'll have the same name as their children. Those who prefer to change back to their maiden name should do so as early as possible to avoid duplicating paperwork (that is, if you're going to open a new credit card you might as well do it under your new name).

SEASONED SINGLES (FOR EXPERIENCED VETERANS)

You've been in the trenches awhile, and you don't need me to tell you that survival is a tough teacher. Somewhere along the way you've lost your dream. Or maybe you still find some pleasure in the daily joys, but you can't get a handle on the future. Don't get caught in the trap of "I've been doing this myself. Nobody else understands. Nobody else can help me." Beware the limiting thought that "I've been coping this way; this is what works for me, I can't try anything new." Your challenge: Find the energy to try something new. Your reality: Stuck in the same old grind. Your mantra: I will enact positive change now.

The first step in enacting positive change is to discard limiting patterns. The second is to replace them with healthier patterns. Cognitive psychologists teach that changing your life is as easy (or as difficult) as changing your habitual thoughts. After all, your thoughts affect your feelings and emotions. In turn, your emotions affect your actions and behaviors. Most limiting patterns that hold you back in life and relationships also hold you back financially. For example, believing that there is never enough can become a self-fulfilling prophecy.

What are some limiting patterns more specific to finances? Spending to save: "This $200 sweater is 50 percent off... I'll save $100!" Defeatist attitudes: "I've already blown my budget today, so I might as well just give it up for the rest of the week." Blaming: "My parents screwed me up and now I can't earn a good living." Rationalizing: "Even though it's a stretch, if I buy this new car, then I'll save on repair bills and get better gas mileage." Denial: "Why plan for the future, it can't happen to me." Devaluing yourself: "I've never been good at (fill in the blank). You can't teach an old dog new tricks." Try not to let yourself become trapped by similar feelings or behaviors.

NEWLY SINGLE: SUMMARY OF POINTERS

1. Avoid the temptation to change your lifestyle immediately, and recognize the obvious and subtle psychological implications to your newly independent status.

2. Talk about finances with your family. Remember, you're not the only one who may face problems, and to the extent you are comfortable, share your situation with children, parents, and siblings, so they will understand your new position.

3. Learn the fundamentals of financial management to stay in control of your new and old assets.

4. Find and stick with advisors you can trust.

5. With the new responsibilities of single parenting, prepare estate plans, including guardianship and financial provisions for your children. If you made a will with your spouse, update it.

RESOURCES

Melvin, Belli M. Sr., Mel Krantzler & Christopher S. Taylor. *Divorcing.* NY: St. Martin's Press, 1988.

Child Custody Legal Resource Kit, NOW Legal Defense and Education Fund (available from NOW Legal Defense and Education Fund, 99 Hudson Street, New York NY 10013).

Divorce and Separation Legal Resource Kit, NOW Legal Defense and Education Fund (available from NOW Legal Defense and Education Fund, 99 Hudson Street, New York, NY 10013.

Linda D. Elrod. *Child Custody Practice and Procedure.* Deerfield, Ill: Clark Boardman Callaghan, 1993.

Ann Moss. *Your Pension Rights at Divorce: What Women Need to Know.* Wasington, D.C.: Pension Rights Center, 1995. Available for $23.95. Pension Rights Center, 918 16 St. NW, Ste. 704, Wasington, D.C. 20006-2902.

Women and Divorce: Turning Your Life Around, Southampton, NY: National Center for Women and Retirement Research, 1993.

CHAPTER 3

Special Cases

Contrary to popular stereotypes, divorce is not the only road to single parenthood. In 1994, 38 percent of single parents were never married. Another 5 percent were widowed. Fewer still are those whose determination to have children led them to adoption or artificial insemination as a route to parenthood despite their single status.

As much as possible, I have filled this book with advice applicable to any single parent. This chapter takes a brief look at the special issues and concerns of those who don't fit the most common profiles. If you are in one of the categories in this chapter, I salute you for your bravery and strength.

THE NEVER-MARRIED MOTHER

If you find yourself a member of this group, you most commonly became pregnant out of wedlock and decided that's the way you wanted it. If you are in a lower income bracket, society sees you as a menace; a burden. If your earnings are higher, editorialists diagnose you with the "Murphy Brown Syndrome" and question your values. Either way, you have chosen parenthood without a partner.

As the incidence of unwed motherhood has increased, laws have changed to accommodate this growing category of families. Paternity laws require certain responsibilities of the father whether or not he has physical interactions with the children. As you will see in Chapter 9, "The Missing Parent," there are agencies available to help you establish paternity and get child support started. If you are actually living with the father but chose not to marry, some states give you the legal rights of a common law marriage, which affect your other financial affairs as well.

> 30% of births in the US are to unwed mothers, compared to under 4% in 1940.
> —U.S. DEPT. OF HEALTH AND HUMAN SERVICES

> Unwed childbearing is "not a teen problem, not a minority problem and not a poverty problem. We are looking at something society-wide. We have to think much bigger."
> —KIRSTEN A. MOORE, EXECUTIVE DIRECTOR, CHILD TRENDS, INC., WASHINGTON, D.C.

Your financial concerns may not differ dramatically from those of most single parents, but you may be burdened with a negative societal view. Unlike divorce, which has now become mainstream, unwed parenthood is still colored with negative connotations in the media. Studies show that your offspring are more at risk for drug abuse, incarceration, and teenage pregnancy; all expensive propositions for you and other taxpayers.

Don't buy into such dire predictions. Blaming single parents for the ills of society won't cure the problem. Voluntary and governmental intervention to provide support, including fathering and mothering will.

WIDOWS AND WIDOWERS

If you've been faced with the tragedy of a deceased spouse, you already know how difficult it is to balance your need for grieving with the pressing demands of everyday life. Perhaps the most formidable task for the widowed single parent is getting your financial affairs in order—when every decision will be a decision made alone, and every form you fill out will underscore your new status as a single parent.

After the most immediate needs of your spouse's funeral and burial, you'll need to turn to the following pressing financial questions:

Hiring help. No one can replace your spouse. But especially if your spouse was the primary caregiver for your children, you'll need to find a substitute. Paying for services such as driving, cooking, laundry, and childcare can add heavily to your expenses in the first year and beyond.

Death certificate. Be sure to photocopy the certificate, and keep the original in a safe place. Time and again, you'll need it in closing your loved one's financial affairs.

Social Security. If your spouse worked, you're probably entitled to social security benefits for yourself and your

HELPING CHILDREN COPE WITH DEATH

Children move through the same stages of grief that adults do, but they may show it in different ways. Behavioral problems, regression to earlier developmental stages, and even uncharacteristic cheerfulness may all signal a need for help. As a parent, you can provide guidance about more appropriate ways to express feelings.

Signal your support with plenty of physical affection. Model an open expression of feelings through words and actions. Encourage children to speak of their loss, what they loved about their deceased parent, and what they will miss. Use simple language they can understand to identify powerful emotions such as anger, guilt, and fear.

Answer children's questions about death directly and honestly, according to your spiritual beliefs and their age. Children are usually satisfied with a direct simple answer. If they want or need more information, they will ask.

Later, children should be allowed to talk of the deceased parent, recall favorite happy times, or look at pictures to refresh their memories. Although such activities can be bittersweet for you, they can add richly to your children's identity and sense of self.

minor children. In addition, to ensure eligibility for your spouse's retirement benefits, you must apply within two years of the death even if you won't be retiring for years to come. For more information, call the Social Security Administration Monday through Friday 7 a.m. through 7 p.m. (all time zones) (800) 772-1213.

Insurance. Check for policies you might have forgotten about in your time of grief. In addition to your main policy, you might have smaller courtesy policies provided as extras on bank accounts, credit cards, or credit union accounts. If there was no insurance or inadequate insurance, you'll have to take drastic downsizing measures to make ends meet.

Medical bills. If the deceased had a lengthy illness, your medical bills could be staggering. Doctors and hospitals will normally work with you to arrange a realistic payment plan for the part you must pay.

Other bills. If they were joint accounts, you're responsible. Otherwise, a married partner isn't responsible for

> An unwed father will be required to pay child support if a court determines or he acknowledges that he's the father; in addition, he may seek custody or visitation.
> —NOLO'S POCKET GUIDE TO FAMILY LAW

unpaid debts of a deceased spouse. If you kept separate accounts, don't pay off credit cards and other debts from your own funds. Beneficiaries are not responsible for such debts, and should the debts exceed the assets, the creditor must cancel the debt.

ADOPTION AND ARTIFICIAL INSEMINATION

Single parents who adopted or conceived through artificial insemination face their own set of challenges. Though reasons for choosing this path vary, you have invested huge amounts of time and money from the beginning. You might be dealing with adoption or medical expenses for years to come, and facing special challenges in a world whose systems are not set up for their particular family structure.

VICTIMS OF ABUSE

While it is important for both parents to keep involved, victims of spousal abuse or child abuse must follow the advice of your attorney,

GUIDELINES FOR ABUSED SPOUSES AND CHILDREN

If you were or are battered, get help. Cease all interactions with the abuser. You'll be unable to make sound decisions about your future if you're living in fear for your life. There is no excuse for staying in a physically abusive situation. Even if you fear destitution, you'll be doing yourself and your children a favor if you get out now.

Call Childhelp USA/IOF Foresters National Child Abuse Hotline for crisis counseling, child abuse reporting information, and referrals to other national, state, and local agencies. The hotline is staffed by mental health professionals 24 hours a day, seven days a week. 1-800-4-A-CHILD (1-800-422-4453).

The National Committee to Prevent Child Abuse recognizes that high stress levels place single parents at greater risk to perpetuate child abuse. Among other products and services, they offer an excellent brochure, called *Stress and the Single Parent*, that details steps you can take to prevent child abuse in your own family. For a free catalog, contact NCPCA, Publications Dept., P.O. Box 2866, Chicago, IL 60690, 1-800-55-NCPCA (1-800-556-2722).

health professional, or counselor at a shelter for the battered to determine your best course of action.

If your separation or divorce is a result of spousal abuse and/or child abuse within the family, you'll have additional financial concerns as well as mental health issues. Both you and your children will likely find yourselves needing psychotherapy, which is costly.

In addition, this situation may deprive you of the financial and moral support of the other parent, since for obvious reasons, contact may be limited and cooperation scant. Thus, you'll have to make up for financial shortfalls from your earnings or settlement monies if any.

Don't hesitate to seek out special community programs aimed at your family. As a society, we have become more aware of the pervasiveness of abuse. Even if you're otherwise financially capable, don't short-circuit this needed healing for financial (or emotional) reasons. Studies show that the victims of abuse become abusers. To break this behavioral chain, you must take it on yourself to help yourself and your children heal.

When you or your child are in personal danger, wage garnishment is the only acceptable method of collecting child support. While you should check with your attorney about a restraining order, many have shied away from this potentially life saving move because of the perceived expense. Either in addition or instead, file for a free protective order through your district attorney's office.

RESOURCES

See Appendix 1: Accessing Government Financial Assistance

Alexandra Armstrong and Mary R. Donahue. *On Your Own: A Widow's Passage to Emotional & Financial Well-Being.* Chicago: Dearborn Financial Publishing, Inc., 1993.

Joyce Brothers. *Widowed.* New York: Simon & Schuster, 1990.

Phyllis Burke. *Family Values: Two Moms and Their Son.* New York: Random House, 1993.

Philomene Gates. *Suddenly Alone: A Woman's Guide to Widowhood.* New York: Harper & Row, 1990.

CHAPTER 4

Setting Financial Goals

Whether you're suffering the loss of a spouse through divorce or death, it's hard to set new goals when you're busy wishing that old situations would reinstate themselves. Until you go through the stages of grief, you'll be stuck bemoaning the past instead of planning the future. It helps to look at the literature on grief to guide us toward understanding the process.

You must give yourself time. I remember the first year after my separation all too well. My first impulse vacillated between immediate replacement of my husband and denying that he wasn't coming back. The perfect solution for both these states of mind would be to attend our church's grief seminar, so when I received encouragement from a caring minister, I enrolled. I thought I might find men to meet as well as start to accept my life. As the evening proceeded, I finally went to the organizer and told her that I absolutely wasn't in the same position as the other people in the room. My situation was only temporary, and I didn't need to go through this seminar. Classic denial—but I didn't even recognize it, despite the posting of the list in the box.

Think of grieving for a lost mate this way: If you had a leg or arm amputated, the U.S. government's Veteran's Affairs gives you two years to recover. Surely loosing a mate, where there was love and children involved, would be worse than loosing an arm or a leg, from a psychological point of view. You must allow yourself ample time to recover before you do too much. But sometime during the first year or so, you'll

STAGES OF GRIEF

1. Shock, Denial
2. Anger, Guilt
3. Bargaining
4. Depression
5. Acceptance

find yourself with true inner inklings that a change has occurred, rather than with lip service to the external changes.

Once the stages have been experienced, you're ready to make a clean break and to start over. All along the way, the steps you take to bring your life under control will also help work through the grieving process, bringing you to acceptance. For me—and I hope for you—acceptance signals a point where you're ready to actively re-build your life, including most important here, your financial life.

You've spent the last few chapters exploring who you are on the single-parent continuum and where you are financially speaking. Now it's time to decide where you want to be and how to get there.

MAKING IT HAPPEN

Even single parents who aren't experiencing an immediate loss of a loved one through divorce or death will benefit from these exercises to help get rid of extra baggage from the past, so they can focus on the future.

On learning of the title of this book, one single mother quipped, "Money is God." Interpretation: Money is a key factor in our daily lives. Our money management today has a direct effect on our future financial security. But greater forces beyond our control can make us or break us despite our best efforts. Our only defense here is to prepare well for contingencies and to hope that they never happen.

Try not to be intimidated by the financial planning process. After all, if you've got basic checking and savings accounts, insurance, or a home, you've already done your share of financial planning

EXERCISE 1: A Fresh Canvas, Letting Go of the Past

Set aside about an hour of private time, and prepare to be completely honest with yourself for maximum benefit.

1. Think back as far as your memory can go, and write down all the losses that come to mind.

a. First, focus on those losses you experienced as a child. What messages did you get from parents and others regarding loss and how to handle it? Write down these messages.

b. Now, bring to mind your current loss and write a brief description of how those messages have affected your dealing with it.

2. Go back to the beginning of the relationship you have currently lost. Think about the good times and the bad times, that is, those events that stand out for you in either category.

a. Make a list of each.

b. Briefly write what you wish you had said but left unsaid in relation to each event.

3. Find your own way to let go of feelings that keep you stuck in the past. This may be as easy as writing them down as you have done here, expressing them to a close friend or counselor, or making a symbolic gesture such as burning the paper they are written on and watching your regrets "go up in smoke."

Adapted from a similar exercise in A New Beginning Loss Workshop held by Mary Garbezi at the First United Methodist Church of Santa Monica, California.

EXERCISE 2: Painting Your Dream

1. Find a quiet spot where you can think. Many parents may find that this task requires locking themselves in the bathroom or setting the alarm to wake an hour earlier. With pen in hand, set a timer for ten minutes, and jot down everything you want for yourself in life. Put your rational mind on the back burner, and let yourself explore completely unfettered, as if you're a child daydreaming in school. Your list may include serious items such as an education for yourself or your children to more light-hearted entries such as a paradise island vacation. Goals could be as small as getting a weekly manicure or as large as moving to a different city and enrolling at a university. No holds barred!

2. When the timer goes off, it's time to take stock. Faced with a huge list of dreams, you could become paralyzed at the impossibility of achieving

them all. You'll need to pare down the list, so that you are working on only one or two major goals at a time. Choose the 10 goals that are most important to you, and copy those on a blank sheet of paper. Don't throw away your master list. You'll have fun referring to it in the future as well as using it to remind you of what you're working for.

3. Number your 10 goals in order of importance to you, and copy them in the new order on a separate sheet of paper. Writing down your priorities is the first step toward achieving them.

Now that you have painted your dreams, you may be frustrated by your current financial reality and wonder how you could ever achieve them. While the steps toward achieving your goals will be tempered by the realities of your current budget, you have far more control than you realize. Just think of each action you take as a potential step toward your goals or away from them. Ask yourself each day, "does this thought/action/ feeling contribute one more brushstroke on my dream painting, or am I figuratively pouring turpentine all over the canvas by taking this step?" In a nutshell: Don't allow yourself to feel limited by your current reality. Instead, focus on the dream and make sure your actions carry you in the right direction.

It is important to take stock every year or two to determine how your needs have changed. Keep your written exercises for comparison. It will be interesting to note whether goals that seemed so important at the time are lower priorities later, and if a goal is still important, you'll detect whether you have strayed from the original plan and then be able to rechart your course.

Give yourself space to draft your own goals. In my legal practice, I give this same advice to married couples, and it applies doubly to you. Leave your significant other or the missing parent out of the equation for a moment while you set down your own goals. After all, you're the only one whose actions you can be sure of. The time for discussion with family, loved ones, and your child's other parent is after you're clear with yourself. If you have a significant other or older children, you can ask them to draft their own goals, then come together for thoughtful discussion. While goals may initially appear discordant, a respectful negotiation will usually result in a unified set of plans for your family.

EXERCISE 3: The Worksheet

After you set down your general dreams, you should divide them into manageable steps. Start by listing goal number one from your dream list on a separate sheet of paper (use the worksheet that follows as a guideline). Determine if it is short term (less than a month), medium term (less than a year), and long term (a year and beyond). List the steps necessary to achieve it, including guidelines on how much to set aside in your budget (more on budgeting in Chapter 5). Most important, set dates to complete each task. Check off and date the steps as you complete them. As you're working on each goal, hang the worksheet in a location where you'll see it each morning to help keep you focused on your objective. Include at least one step that you can complete immediately and do it!

RESOURCES

Janet Bamford, Jeff Blyskal, Emily Card, Aileen Jacobson with Greg Daugherty. *The Consumer Reports Money Book: How to Get It, Save It, and Spend it Wisely*. 3rd. ed. Yonkers, NY: Consumer Reports Books, 1995.

John James and Frank Cherry. *The Grief Recovery Handbook: A Step-by-Step Program for Moving Beyond Loss*. New York: Harper & Row, 1988.

MAKE IT HAPPEN WORKSHEET

Today's Date: May 13, 1997

Describe the goal or objective in detail: Set aside emergency funds for three months' worth of bare bones living expenses in a savings account.

Is it short, medium, or long term? (For larger goals, it may be necessary to do a separate worksheet for each smaller step.) *Medium term.*

WHAT STEPS ARE NECESSARY TO ACHIEVE IT?	TO BE COMPLETED BY:	ACTUAL:
1. Determine my minimum monthly expenses.	Date: *Today*	*5/13/97*
2. Open a savings account and make my first deposit.	Date:	*5/15/97*
3. Budget periodic deposits into my account.	Date:	*5/15/97*

What is the total cost of this objective? *$4,800.*

Over what period will I allocate funds to meet this objective? *One year.*

What method will I use to allocate the funds? *To save $4,800 in one year, I will need to set aside $400 per month. Since I am paid bimonthly, I will set up a $200 bank draft from my checking account to my savings account on the 1st and 15th of each month, remembering to note the withdrawals in my checkbook register accordingly. After I have met my goal, I'll be free to redirect the $400 per month into higher risk investments or other special projects.*

PART TWO

Strategies for Getting There

CHAPTER 5

Counting on Yourself

With goals in hand, you should realize that all parents want the best for their children, but before you can give to your children, you must take care of yourself. Some single parents put their children's needs front and center, ignoring their own adult requirements of nourishment and growth. The following airlines standard emergency instructions apply to you: Put on your own oxygen mask first before helping the children. Although this approach is hard to accept, you must protect yourself to have energy to protect your children.

As if you didn't have enough troubles, you may find your former spouse vying for the children's attention with treats you can't afford. One Los Angeles woman told of her husband arriving in a chauffeured limousine for play dates with his child, while the mother had never ridden in a limousine in her life. Opportunistic children have been known to play on this competitive tendency, trying to fill the void caused by their confusion over the family breakup. Though you may be tempted to play this game, turn it around by helping yourself and your child view these extra goodies as bonuses but not the usual budget entries.

Let go of the guilt. Your child's dance lessons can wait until next week. This week you'll learn the budgeting strategies you need to pay bills and to save for the things you really want, so you can be on the road to solvency and success.

SUPERPARENT SYNDROME

As a child visiting my grandmother's farm, I soon learned that if we used too much well water, the well would appear to go dry. After a rest, the well could be primed by adding a little bucket of water kept handy for this purpose. Priming would bring up the water level just enough for the pump to start, and the water would flow again. The lesson: With a little regular attention in the first place, the well would continue to give water. If your own "pump" needs priming, you're probably going to be the one who has to do it.

Remember, in the well story, the water is always there. A little TLC gets it flowing again. You have a well of strength inside too. A few "don'ts" will help you cope with your seemingly insurmountable responsibilities as a single parent: Don't let guilt over the breakup or your financial shortcomings defeat you. Don't be afraid to call on friends and relatives for help and moral support. Don't be ashamed to lower your standards a little. Don't expect to do everything perfectly when you've got so much to do.

Parent Pampering

Counteract or avoid burnout by taking care of yourself regularly. Learn how to find hidden moments to treat yourself. On the weekends, rather than cleaning the house when your children are napping, take a nap yourself or try one of the following hints. If you have an hour for lunch, take a few minutes for light exercise at a nearby health club, take a stroll, or find a quiet spot to eat a sandwich and to read a few chapters in a novel. You may have your own favorite ways to relax and unwind. The following ideas have worked for others:

> **Earth:** Although gardening isn't for everyone, many find a special joy in kneeling in the warm earth on a spring day to plant growing things. Others find a similar connection to nature by growing houseplants or indoor herb gardens.

> **Air:** Take a stroll by yourself to collect yourself. Fresh air does wonders if you take the time to breath it in and experience the sights, smells, and sounds around you. Even if the weather isn't pristine, try to experience it through a child's eyes. Your two-year-old wouldn't stiffen and cower from a light rain. Instead, she would revel in the gentle wet drops on her cheeks.

Fire: To my co-author's trailblazing grand-mother, there's nothing more relaxing than staring into a flickering campfire until it's reduced to embers. Fire appeals to our basic instincts for warmth and energy. At home, without a fireplace, she loves to light candles for that mellow and gentle lighting that can make any day into a special occasion.

STRESSBUSTERS ALERT

Never automatically read your mail or turn on the TV when you first get home.

Water: Swimming, hot candlelit bubble baths, and whirl-pool baths work wonders if there's someone to watch the kids. If not, make it a quick shower or a family romp in the sprinkler system on a sunny afternoon.

Other tips for unwinding after a busy day include:

1. Short, simple exercise sessions to keep up your energy level. Try jogging, swimming, or bicycling with your children. Or, do simple yoga stretches with them:

    Rotate your shoulders slowly, first forward, then backward.

    Raise your arms slowly above your head while breathing in, stretch them out, and exhale as you bring them down.

    Bend from the waist and hang quietly as long as comfortable, then come up slowly. If you're very stiff you can stand in front of a table or chair and bend over until your hands reach it. Let your head hang and close your eyes

2. Occasional "spa treats" like a massage, haircut, facial, man-icure, or pedicure. Even men will enjoy the foot massage that goes along with a good pedicure. If a massage is too expensive have your children give you a backrub. One mom gives her two preschoolers a bottle of lotion and lets them play with their miniature cars, making "lotion tracks" all over her back.

3. Cuddle with your children while you read a book out loud to them (or let them read out loud to you).

If you take good care of yourself, you'll be better equipped to handle the tough times that happen to all of us. In addition, we've all heard of the studies that show that stress is linked with higher incidences of disease and lower immune response. Therefore, choosing to take care of yourself now can save time, money, and medical expenses later. Take special care during holidays and other family events when emotions are high.

HOLIDAY INSANITY

Even when parents are cooperating, holidays are the worst times for the divorced. We remember the good times, not the bad, and cozy, sentimental ads and music don't help. I expressed my frustrations with the season to a member of a "perfect" family who I thought must have absolutely perfect holidays. The response he gave me was: "What's a holiday without a family fight?" Indeed.

As the custodial parent by default, I became ill enough to spend New Year's in the hospital the first year of my separation. Determined to avoid the grim realities of a sad child and the forced cheer of the season, the next year, off we went to Hawaii. I packed a bag filled with toys and got help from the hotel staff in hiding it. The holiday was relaxed and peaceful, without too much homesickness. The following year, in a budget-minded mood, my travel agent, Sylvia, found me a great deal to Cancun, airfare and hotel included. Usually not one to choose packages, I took the leap. Except for the long wait at LAX, I had a terrific vacation. Waldo, however, was another story. He complained almost nonstop that he didn't like Mexico as much as he'd liked Hawaii. The only break in the whining came on our outing to the Mayan ruins of Chitzenitzen, where Waldo's own heritage fascinated him. While adults laboriously climbed the main pyramid, Waldo ran up and down the very high steps three times.

But on New Year's, the angst returned. The next year, I had almost forgotten how determined Waldo was to stay home until I reread his Cancun New Year's resolutions. Right at the top of the list: Spend Christmas at home. Next—see more of Juju (his dog).

And so this Christmas, Waldo made big plans. He wanted to stay home, but he had a modest Christmas list. Until the visit from Kent, the first time Waldo had seen his father at the holidays in four years.

When Dad arrived, Waldo's wish list was simple, to enjoy the visiting dog and to get a board game or two. He had decided to trim his wants because his intentions included a new CD-ROM computer as soon as our budget allowed.

One very busy day during Kent's visit, I tried to suggest that the two of them visit Sears and look at tools and other "man-type" toys. Stashed away was a battery-operated screwdriver and drill. I thought Waldo might enjoy a work-table to go with it.

Instead, on the last day of his visit, Kent managed to take Waldo to an expensive toy store. Waldo came back with a new wish list.

Waldo presented me with the list three days before Christmas, and I asked our teenage tutor to help me with the shopping, never guessing that we were talking about a $600 plus endeavor. She returned with the airplane, since it alone exhausted the already overbudget $280 I gave her for shopping. And now came the real struggle.

Uncertain whether Santa Claus could get all the toys, Waldo decided to write his plea (see handwritten letter).

I was floored. I faxed the letter to Kent, hoping for help, since he had started this monster-ball rolling. No help from that direction. Finally, I decided to go to the toy store, thinking that I would get what I could. Wouldn't you know it, the Predator, now first on the list, was sold out?

With all the other presents under the tree, Santa left Waldo a reply (see box).

On Christmas, as he opened his presents, Waldo looked all around for the missing car, thinking that he would still find it. Finally, he found Santa's letter in his stocking, and the next several hours were devoted to his vacillating between keeping the plane or swapping it, while lobbying for the car as an "extra." Gosh—I thought I had made a pretty good Christmas at home, but after a few hours of this response, I collapsed. I couldn't face going to dinner with my sister's family as planned, so Waldo went alone to enjoy the Christmas meal. While he was away, I slept, having exhausted myself with trips to the mall and wrapping

Dear Santa,

We haven't been home for
Christmas the last two years,
It must have been hard to find
the Great Waldo. I didn't want
much the last two years but now
I know what I want for Christmas
I would like a Tyco X Treme
Racing set. Next I would like a
Romote controlled car, it's called The
Predator if their is any more colors
then blue don't pick them because
I would like the blue car. The
next gift I would like is the
game Weapons+ Warriors the
Castle combat set. Last but
not Least I would like a Cox
Lectro Electric Powered Radio
Controlled Airplane, that is an
option gift instead if that's to
expensive I'd like my train fixed,
to make it run like new. That's
my list this year Santa and We'll
remember to give you milk and cookies.

page 1

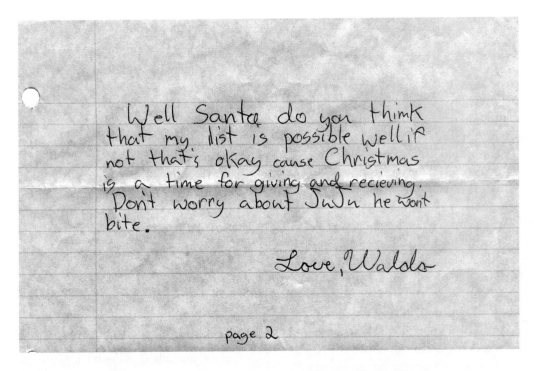

Well Santa do you think that my list is possible well if not that's okay cause Christmas is a time for giving and recieving. Don't worry about JuJu he wont bite.

Love, Waldo

page 2

presents. This blurry end to a not-so-perfect day had me fantasizing about another tropical Christmas. Something about being away makes the holidays easier for me—a sort of unplugged holiday. But I also felt guilty because I realized that Waldo's memory of "Christmas tradition" was limited to the two holidays spent abroad. We hadn't even decorated a tree for the past three years, so Waldo barely remembered our ornament collection, some of which I had kept for 25 years.

How will we solve the holiday choice next time? It's too soon to tell, but right now I'm fantasizing about an African safari.

Of course, my holiday woes pale in comparison with the many single parents who have few choices, if any. While I realize how very fortunate I am to have a career that offers some financial security and some freedom, I believe my feelings, if not the practical realities, parallel those of those less fortunate who face holidays without the "family fight."

Worse still for many parents is the prospect of the holidays without their child. Where joint custody dictates a kid exchange at holiday time,

Dear Waldo,

I have read your list carefully. You have been a very fine person this past year, and I want to make you happy. In thinking about how big and responsible you have become, I have decided to give you the airplane instead of the car. This year I must limit this type of toy, and the airplane is more grown-up and more expensive. If you really want the car, I can let your mother know how to exchange the airplane. I am also thinking you'll like to fly the airplane on trips to the desert and Sacramento.

I am very proud you are going to New Roads School. I know you will do very well. Don't ever be afraid to talk or ask questions just as you were not afraid to ask for the toys you wanted. I really appreciated your fine letter.

Here's a very Merry Christmas to you and your mother.

Love from Santa Claus

the normal custodian feels especially denied, since he or she gets all of the day-to-day pain and little of the vacation pleasure.

Also, whether at the holidays or at other times, the Christmas list episode illustrates how disastrously one parent can be affected by the unthinking actions of the other. My former spouse had no negative intentions in taking Waldo to the store in the first place. But Kent was being Kent—creating a situation, then leaving me to solve it.

Whether your spouse is cooperative or cunning, family trust is hard to maintain when incidents such as these occur. Single parenthood doesn't have to be this way. Children love presents, but they often think of your time with them as the most special present of all. A single dad remarked, "We don't do much in the way of presents, but we do a lot of celebrating, and the kids think it's fun that we celebrate Hanukkah, Christmas, *and* the [winter] solstice. They stay up with me on New Year's, too, and this year Anna got to toot her sax when zero hour arrived as Michael beat on his drums and I banged pots and pans. It was great fun."

Restoring Sanity to Holidays, Vacations, Birthdays, and Other Gift-Giving Occasions

What do you do when your children have become accustomed to high-ticket items? You must emphasize the wealth of experience rather than the wealth of your pocketbook. Create your own traditions as a single-parent family. Otherwise, you may be tempted to fill the void of the missing parent with store-bought goodies that will break your heart as well as your budget. These guidelines will help keep your budget and your sanity intact.

Use special foods to set apart occasions. While I may not recall what Santa brought me on a particular year, I have fond memories of baking and decorating sugar cookies from scratch from my mother's recipe every Christmas Eve. Special foods don't have to be complicated; in fact, the simpler the better for busy single parents. This might mean store-bought refrigerator dough that you roll out and decorate yourself.

Rediscover traditional celebrations such as lighting advent candles, making dreidles, attending midnight mass, or hanging mistletoe.

Make your own holiday traditions. Julie Evans had a long-standing tradition of hanging mistletoe at Christmas that went back to her Irish grandmother. But after her divorce, she simply couldn't afford extras. She tied a red bow around broccoli florets and hung that instead. It was a jolly hit with the kids and became standard operating procedure, even after they could afford the real thing. In solemn contrast, a widower took his three children to visit their mother's grave on holidays. The children placed items of natural beauty such as shells, pinecones, and wildflowers on the grave. In this way they honored the memory of their mother and kept her spirit alive in their hearts. After the children grew up and moved to distant cities, returning home for the holidays had a deeper meaning to them. These examples show that personal traditions can add a richness to our experience that can't be replaced by expensive trinkets.

Celebrate your children's birthdays with fun and inexpensive parties. My co-author's daughter Arabella's first birthday was a celebration of her life. Mom gave her great-grandmother Anne's sewing basket and asked each guest to bring a small note or symbolic trinket to place in the basket. A special ceremony gave each guest the opportunity to explain the message on his or her note, whether it be a serious blessing, a hope for her future, or a humorous anecdote. The basket will be presented to Arabella when she becomes a teenager, when she really needs the support and guidance of her loved ones. Everyone agreed it was a simple yet very special occasion. Here are some guidelines for more traditional children's parties:

SANTA IS COMING TO MOM'S HOUSE THIS YEAR

It was a tough year for Andrea Poole, who had emerged from a nasty divorce with joint custody of her two sons, though they resided primarily with her. Their standard of living dropped dramatically with no property settlement, and child support payments that were sporadic at best. Her mistake was common; sharing a single divorce lawyer with her husband that had left the final decree weighted sharply in his favor. In a calculated move to make the post divorce holiday season even harder, her ex had told the children that "Santa is coming to Mom's house this year." This left her with the extra burden of keeping the Christmas dream alive for seven-year-old Alex and two-year-old Janie. She had to scrounge and save and "couldn't even participate in the $10 teacher's gift exchange," at the elementary school where she taught. Accordingly, she didn't buy a single Christmas gift for anyone. And if it hadn't been for her children's beloved baby-sitter, she wouldn't have had a thing under the tree for herself. The ex's final blow? He bought the boys bicycles for Christmas, "from Dad." He made a big deal over how he had worked so hard to afford them. Andrea couldn't give any parallel gifts from herself. Her efforts had all gone into the "Santa fund." The boys would never know how much she had sacrificed to give them a good Christmas, and she had been "one-upped" by her ex once again in the expensive competition for her children's love.

Limit guests to one per each year of your child's age. For example, a three-year-old will enjoy sharing his or her cake and ice cream with three buddies.

Play simple age appropriate games. They can be competitive (pin the tail on the donkey) or noncompetitive (ring around the rosy).

Let the children do a simple craft related to the party theme. For instance, if it's a Batman party, make Batman masks out of black construction paper. Consult Linda Hetzer's *50 Fabulous Parties for Kids* (see resources).

BUDGETING BASICS

A written budget can make your bottom line more tangible and create concrete spending plans to help you achieve your goals. Communicating these plans to your kids will help motivate them to work with you.

Some of us spent our money conservatively, creating savings. For others, expenses outstrip incomes. We all face the temptation to enjoy life now and spend all the money we make. There are also events that force us to go into debt, such as illness, loss of job, or unexpected expenses. Too many have used credit to close the gap between income and spending, keeping standards high—often at the expense of real prosperity.

Our culture too often promotes the notion that spending money we don't have is a substitute for wealth. Advertising urges middle-class people to consume at levels appropriate to those with wealth, not those who are in the middle of building it. The best way to make money is to conserve it. Rethink your strategies if you formed your investment and spending habits during an inflationary period, when it made sense to use credit and pay later in rapidly declining dollars. The right path during a slower growth cycle resembles a 1930s conservation mentality more than a 1980s consumption one.

If you haven't formed wealth-building habits yet, you can start by applying cash-flow management techniques and conserving your cash. The starting point: Your monthly household budget. You'll get more tips on saving money and changing your lifestyle to meet your needs in future chapters. For now, let's concentrate on budgeting basics.

Americans save an average of only 4.2 percent of disposable income, compared to the average 14.9 percent saved by the Japanese.
SOURCE: U.S. DEPT. OF COMMERCE.

Budget as a Successful Business Would

Although 99 percent of successful businesses in one survey regularly budgeted their expenditures, the same study showed that only 60 percent of individual consumers used budgets, and then only sporadically. You must learn to set up your household like a successful business. After all, you too have "payables" and "receivables." Why not think of your kids as "employees" with "benefits." Get the idea? All the elements are there.

After setting your goals in Chapter 4, you're halfway there. A budget will simply help you reduce those same goals to numerical benchmarks. It can help you achieve the means to buy a new car, afford a special vacation, or begin saving for retirement. Most important, budgeting can be the starting point for prosperity.

Watch out your own psychology can get in the way. People fool themselves about money and how they are using it. Even for people who do budget, temptations are constant. Stores are set up to maximize profit opportunities derived from shoppers' habits. Food items you do not need are placed at eye level in attractive, colorful displays to encourage purchases; staples are at ground level. The checkout counter is the most desirable product location in the supermarket, for consumers add last-minute purchases there and tend not to check the prices as closely as they would in the aisles. Anyone who's watched Saturday morning cartoons with their children know the effect commercials have in the cereal aisle at the grocery store.

If all your income is being used to meet expenses, you won't have room to set aside money for your new goals. Assuming steady income, what changes in spending patterns do you need to make to meet your goals? Whether your goal is to stop depending on credit cards to buy groceries or to purchase a new car, you must start with an examination of your basic budget needs. Basic budgeting is a three step process.

1. *Examine current spending habits.* Look through your receipts, checkbook register, and credit card statements to establish your personal spending categories. Choose major categories of expenses and project how much you need to allocate each month. Fixed expenses like rent or cable bills are easy to list. Variable expenses such as groceries and long distance charges will be harder, and you may need to research your current habits averaging several months of receipts. Again, your categories will depend on your lifestyle. For example,

if restaurant meals are a necessity of your work, they may merit a category of their own. If you eat out only as an occasional treat, you could count your restaurant expenses (along with movie tickets, etc.) under a general heading like entertainment. Keep it as simple as you can.

2. *Set new spending goals.* Determine where you are overspending and project new spending goals for those categories. If you want to cut total spending by $200 per month, you should divvy it up between several categories. For example, a $50 cut in groceries, a $100 cut in wardrobe spending, and a $50 cut in entertainment. Chapter 7 will discuss tips on spending less in these categories.

3. *Track your progress monthly.* Take the time to fill in your ledger when you pay your bills each month. Tabulate your receipts for each category and note how closely your actual spending met your goals. For example, if you allocated $100 per month for restaurant meals and your receipts showed that you spent $90, you'd get a +$10 variance. On the other hand, if you spent $110, you'd have a -$10 variance.

BUDGET WORKSHEETS

Listed here are types of expenses you may incur as a single parent. Your own budget may not be so detailed, or you may find that you need to add additional categories to fit your unique situation. It's helpful to convert all expenditures to monthly amounts for comparison. If your car insurance is paid in a lump sum each year, divide by twelve to find a monthly budget amount. If you dole out your children's allowance weekly, multiply by 52 weeks (weeks in a year) to get the yearly amount and then divide that figure by 12 to get the monthly amount. Finally, for quarterly payments, multiply by four to get the yearly amount and then divide by twelve to get the monthly amount.

Budget Worksheet: Monthly Expenditures

ITEM	CURRENT AMOUNT	TARGET AMOUNT	DIFFERENCE
1. Housing			
Mortgage or rent	$	$	$
Property taxes	$	$	$
Insurance	$	$	$
Utilities	$	$	$
Yard maintenance	$	$	$
Phone	$	$	$
Household purchases and supplies	$	$	$
House cleaning and household help	$	$	$
Home improvements	$	$	$
Other housing costs	$	$	$
Subtotal, housing	*$*	*$*	*$*
2. Food			
Home	$	$	$
Restaurant	$	$	$
Children's lunches	$	$	$
Work lunches	$	$	$

Budget Worksheet: Monthly Expenditures (continued)

ITEM	CURRENT AMOUNT	TARGET AMOUNT	DIFFERENCE
2. Food (continued)			
Warehouse club or food co-op membership	$	$	$
Other	$	$	$
Subtotal, food	*$*	*$*	*$*
3. Clothing			
You	$	$	$
Children	$	$	$
Subtotal, clothing	*$*	*$*	*$*
4. Transportation			
Lease or car note payments	$	$	$
Insurance	$	$	$
Fuel	$	$	$
Maintenance	$	$	$
Other transportation	$	$	$
Subtotal, transportation	*$*	*$*	*$*

Budget Worksheet: Monthly Expenditures (continued)

ITEM	CURRENT AMOUNT	TARGET AMOUNT	DIFFERENCE
5. Dependent Care			
Daycare	$	$	$
Baby-sitter	$	$	$
Summer programs	$	$	$
Support of relatives/others	$	$	$
Other	$	$	$
Subtotal, dependent care	*$*	*$*	*$*
6. Education/school tuition and fees			
You	$	$	$
Children	$	$	$
College savings	$	$	$
Subtotal, school	*$*	*$*	*$*
7. Healthcare			
Well childcare, immunizations	$	$	$
Health insurance premiums	$	$	$
Medicines	$	$	$

Budget Worksheet: Monthly Expenditures (continued)

ITEM	CURRENT AMOUNT	TARGET AMOUNT	DIFFERENCE
7. Healthcare (continued)			
Dental care	$	$	$
Eye care	$	$	$
Subtotal, healthcare	*$*	*$*	*$*
8. Insurance not listed above			
Disability	$	$	$
Life	$	$	$
Other	$	$	$
Subtotal, insurance	*$*	*$*	*$*
9. Recreation/entertainment			
Your club memberships	$	$	$
Children's club memberships	$	$	$
Magazine/newspaper subscriptions	$	$	$
Zoo/museum/park memberships	$	$	$
Personal care and improvements	$	$	$
Vacations/travel	$	$	$

Budget Worksheet: Monthly Expenditures (continued)

ITEM	CURRENT AMOUNT	TARGET AMOUNT	DIFFERENCE
9. Recreation/entertainment (continued)			
Hobbies	$	$	$
Movies and video rentals	$	$	$
Other	$	$	$
Subtotal, recreation	*$*	*$*	*$*
10. Goodwill			
Gifts, children	$	$	$
Gifts, others	$	$	$
Charitable contributions	$	$	$
Children's allowances	$	$	$
Subtotal, goodwill	*$*	*$*	*$*
11. Consumer credit debt reduction			
Mastercard	$	$	$
Visa	$	$	$
American Express	$	$	$

Budget Worksheet: Monthly Expenditures (continued)

ITEM	CURRENT AMOUNT	TARGET AMOUNT	DIFFERENCE
11. Consumer credit debt reduction (continued)			
Discover	$	$	$
Gas cards	$	$	$
Department store	$	$	$
Other	$	$	$
Subtotal, debt reduction	*$*	*$*	*$*
12. Retirement plans (other than those automatically deducted from your salary)			
IRA	$	$	$
Other	$	$	$
Subtotal, *retirement plans*	*$*	*$*	*$*
13. Taxes			
Federal income tax	tax	$	$
State income tax	$	$	$
Social security/ FICA	$	$	$
State disability/ unemployment	$	$	$
Subtotal, taxes	*$*	*$*	*$*

COUNTING ON YOURSELF   57

Budget Worksheet: Monthly Expenditures (continued)

ITEM	CURRENT AMOUNT	TARGET AMOUNT	DIFFERENCE
14. Other expenses not listed above			
Investment (payments to savings, etc.)	$	$	$
Petty cash	$	$	$
Miscellaneous	$	$	$
Subtotal, other expenses	*$*	*$*	*$*
TOTAL EXPENDITURES (ADD SUBTOTALS)	*$*	*$*	*$*

Budget Worksheet: Income

ITEM		
1. Gross income* from employment, less deductions such as dependent care and 401(k) contributions.		
Salary	$	
Commissions	$	
Self-Employment	$	

Budget Worksheet: Income (continued)

ITEM		
1. Gross income* from employment, less deductions such as dependant care and 401(k) contributions. (continued)		
Other	$	
Subtotal, employment		**$**
2. Income from other parent		
Alimony	$	
Child support	$	
Social Security	$	
Life insurance benefits	$	
Subtotal, income from other parent		**$**
3. Investment income		
Taxable interest	$	
Nontaxable interest	$	
Dividends	$	
Rents	$	
Investment partnerships	$	
Trust fund	$	
Other	$	
Subtotal, investments	**000**	
TOTAL EXPENDITURES (ADD SUBTOTALS)		**$**

*Use your gross income here because taxes are deducted from your expenditure worksheet.

Of course, not every penny can be tracked. Give yourself some slack with a petty cash or miscellaneous fund. You may only need to do this exercise for a few months while you gain control. Provided that you take time to track your actual expenses, you'll build an awareness of whether you're meeting your target spending amounts. If not, you may need to examine the reality of your budget and readjust your goals. Eventually, it should become a mental process with a daily awareness of where you stand.

PAY YOURSELF FIRST

Make savings a fixed expense on your budget (from 5-10 percent of your income depending on your debt ratio). Have the money deducted before you even miss it in a payroll savings plan or even a monthly bankdraft from your checking to savings account.

TECHNIQUES

Most of us have tried budgeting, failed, and tried again. Choosing a method suited to your personality and the level of financial complication in your life will help keep you on track. Whether you use shoeboxes and notebook paper or sophisticated computer programs and on-line banking, your goal is to gain awareness and control of your spending habits.

Computers have revolutionized our financial lives. As a single parent, you may number among the estimated 40 percent of all households with children that have home computers. In addition to providing the ubiquitous computer games for your kids, your computer can help with daily bookkeeping, tap into on-line banking services such as bill payment, and even complete more sophisticated moves like trading stocks.

For bottom line bookkeeping tasks such as balancing your checkbook and calculating net worth, start with a basic program such as Quicken, the personal and family finance organizer from Intuit or The Budget Kit from Dearborn Publishing.

It is now possible to connect with your local bank and download individual check amounts right into your Quicken database, eliminating the need to enter the records by hand. You may also track your credit card spending by a similar downloading procedure, though not all credit card issuers offer this service.

On-line banking has made great strides since its introduction in the 1980s, but it's still confusing to most. Every software package has glitches, and every area of the country has something different to offer. To further confuse the matter, you may soon bypass direct connections with specific institutions in favor of "one-stop-shopping" on the Internet. This prospect scares some, who worry about security problems and access to their private accounts. But Federal law makes the bank liable for such potential problems, as long as they didn't arise from your negligence. In other words, keep your password secure and you should be fine.

If you're considering hooking up with your financial institution's home banking program, you are probably aware of the fees involved, typically about $15 per month or 50 cents for each bill paid. Although technology is changing rapidly in this area, there are still fundamental problems.

1. *You still can't make deposits or withdraw cash from home.* Upcoming remedies include electronic cash, a magnetized debit card you can load from home with money from your banking account; and electronic checks, which will enable other electronic bankers to deposit money directly into your account without printing anything on paper.

2. *It's slow.* If a creditor doesn't have the capacity for electronic funds transfers, your bank will have to write a check and mail it, just as you would have. Delivery time will be at the mercy of the postal system and the check will arrive without the benefit of a payment coupon, which could cause further delays in crediting your account. If you like to wait until the end of your grace period to pay your mortgage, this method may not be right for you.

Bank account budgeting carries on the analogy of running your home like a business. It's simply a different way to organize your funds and your thinking. If you have made up and dropped many budgets, the answer may lie in instituting controls through a simplified "accounts" system using more than one bank account.

Bank accounts can serve two broad budget categories: current expenses and long-term investments. With a checking account for monthly bills and a money-market or interest-bearing fund for longer-term goals, you can budget by depositing to one account the amount you plan to spend on current expenses.

TAX IMPLICATIONS FOR THE SINGLE PARENT

When you divorce, you may become aware of taxes for the first time if your spouse handled the accounting. Even if you knew your way around your old 1040, new issues arise during and after divorce. Briefly, these include:

1. Alimony is tax deductible to the obligor (payer) and taxable to the payee. That rule means that if you pay alimony, you can deduct it in a very favorable position, above the "adjusted gross income," the figure used to determine if you qualify for other deductions such as medical expenses. If you receive alimony, don't forget to factor in the taxes you will pay on these funds.

2. Child support is not taxable. The obligor may not claim it as a deduction and the payee does not have to report it as income.

3. Dependency deduction—each person in your household is worth a certain amount on your tax return as a deduction. In 1995, the figure stood at $2,500, but it is indexed for inflation, so the number changes annually. If you want the deduction and are sharing custody, be sure to ask for it. The law allows the parties to decide who will take the deduction, so sometimes the argument is made that the higher earner who pays higher taxes should take the deduction. No way—you'll never get enough in child support, so take the deduction and make it part of the settlement. You'll need it.

4. If you provide the principal residence for you children, you will now file as "head of household" which brings you into a more favorable tax bracket than for a single filer.

5. If you sell your home, the law allows you to split the appreciation or gain in equity among the two parties any way you want. That rule allows both of you to buy new (but smaller) homes and use the tax "rollover" or deferment for yourselves.

6. The Earned Income Tax Credit (EITC) is a refundable tax credit for working people who don't earn much money. If you are working and have a child, your EITC is higher. You may find you suddenly qualify for the EITC upon divorce. Check it and take it—it's valuable to you.

7. If you have childcare expenses, make sure to calculate your taxes using both the Dependent Care Tax Credit and the Dependent Care Deduction. For people in low earnings brackets, the credit provides more tax relief. For higher earners, the deduction works better. If the deduction would be better for you, ask your employer to pay your childcare directly because up to $5,000 a year can come straight off your income—and off the amount you're taxed on.

8. Finally, be aware that the IRS can impose "joint and several liability" for tax bills incurred on your "married filing jointly" income tax returns from previous years. Under this provision, both parties are responsible for any tax liabilities they incurred together and haven't paid, any charges due to a fraudulent tax return, and

any charges that occur as a result of a future audit, even if legally divorced at the time of the audit.

For more information on taxes, consult *The Ms. Money Book* (see chapter Resources) and talk with your accountant or tax preparer.

Return to a cash economy to make your spending more concrete. If you don't have the money, you simply have to wait to purchase the desired object. Credit cards have a way of cushioning us from our financial realities. Although checks are generally thought of as cash, we may go days, weeks, or months without balancing our accounts and overdraft protection may give us a misleading feeling of security.

Caution: Bank account budgeting requires discipline, because having investment funds liquid (easily withdrawn) can provide a temptation should overspending occur in the expense account.

As an eye-opening exercise, withdraw cash in your budgeted amount in certain categories. If you've budgeted $50 a week for groceries and you get paid every two weeks, get the $100 grocery money when you deposit your check. Keep it in a separate envelope in your wallet and use it only to buy groceries. After each purchase, stick the change and receipt back in the envelope. If you get to the checkout and you've overspent your limit, don't allow yourself to borrow from other sources of money in your wallet (such as your "gas money," your "haircut" envelope, and especially not your Visa card!). Instead, eliminate some of the frivolous items from your grocery basket right on the spot. Who cares what the

Caution: The "return to the cash economy" exercise is meant to help you spend your cash in a more controlled manner; allowing you to track your spending as well as limit it. One of the dangers of using cash is the difficulty of tracking it. If the temptations of ATM machines seem to wreck your plans, tuck your withdrawal slips in an envelope with your receipts.

cashier thinks, right? This exercise can work well in a single parent household, where you have more control over your cash flow. You may also find this technique useful to curtail your credit spending. Leave that plastic at home.

Purchase order budgeting is for those who cannot bring themselves to budget (or have very little room to change most expenses), but want to cut back on their cash outgo. Prepare a form and use it for all your planned purchases.

To use the form, fill in what you intend to purchase and the price. Think about the purchase and get approval from yourself, as if you worked for a business where the order would have had to be approved by a controller or financial officer.

PURCHASE ORDER FORM

Date   _____

Item   _____

Purpose   _____

Date needed   _____

Estimated cost _____

Discussed with _____

Agreed upon?   _____

Your Annual Financial Checkup

No matter what format or combination of techniques you use, eventually the time will come in your budgeting process for a review. Tax time is a good time, since you've got out all your paperwork already. Give yourself a chance to see how you have done and to set goals for succeeding months or years. You may want to graph debt repayment and savings so you can actually see the debt line fall and the savings line rise. Or you may simply adjust plans for expenditure categories that exceeded their limits. But, before you leave budgeting behind, take time to check how you performed against your original plans. Even if you complete the cycle only once, you will have a better sense of how your spending compares to your plans.

RESOURCES

Emily Card. *The Ms Money Book: Strategies for Prospering in the Coming Decade.* New York: E.P. Dutton, 1990.

Linda Hetzer. *50 Fabulous Parties for Kids.* New York: Crown, 1994.

Roseanne Hirsch. *Super Working Mom's Handbook: Hundreds of Time-Saving, Useful Ideas to Lighten Your Life.* New York: Warner Books, 1986.

McCullough, Bonnie & Bev Cooper. *76 Ways to Get Organized for Christmas And make it special, too*[Sic]. New York: St. Martin's Press, 1982.

Evan Imber-Black, Ph.D. and Janine Robers, Ed.D. *Rituals for Our Times.* New York: HarperCollins, 1992.

CHAPTER 6

A Balancing Act

Because I was always the main breadwinner in my marriage, during the separation I had to replace my husband's contribution to child rearing with paid baby-sitters and drivers. The other alternative was to give up part of my client practice to make more time for my son. Making the tough choices took time and thought.

Being a single parent in today's economic climate involves financial and time trade-offs. Even in the most ideal situations, when parents are getting along and child support is flowing regularly, the custodial parent must avoid being lulled into a false sense of security. The overall financial goal of every single parent should be to earn enough to survive without child support payments.

This strategy has a two-pronged approach. First, stick to lifestyle choices that align with your child-rearing values. Are the $150 sneakers that your child wants worth the extra hours you'll have to work (and be away from your child) to pay for them? Second, find cost effective ways to increase your income. You may need to change jobs, get a job if you didn't have one, or start a side business. In any case, use our "Working Smarter" guidelines to help you squeeze more time from the hours you devote to working.

If child support does come, if at all possible, think of it as "icing on the cake." Save it or use it to buy deferred items, but don't depend on it. Caution: Refer to your financial road map before spending extra dollars. Be aware of the "trickle down" effect of frittering away a few cents here a few dollars there. Bottom line: Balance your discretionary income between splurge items such as a vacation and serious goals such as education and retirement.

EARNING MORE VERSUS SPENDING TIME WITH THE KIDS

The American dream tells us that no matter how much you earn, you can always earn more by working harder. We focus so much on increasing our incomes because we assume that it's the way to solve our financial woes. Unfortunately, it's just as common for people with six-figure incomes to file bankruptcy as it is for those making the middle-class average of $30,000. This example illuminates the misplaced emphasis we set on earning more that keeps us trapped in a "buy now, pay later, after all I'll be making more by then" mind-set. If we could shift some of that emphasis to the idea of living within our means no matter what it is, we'd be happier and enjoy more time with our families.

Many single parents have been caught in a survival struggle; working more and more hours away from their children simply to pay the bills and put food on the table; all the while feeling guilty for missing out on important milestones in their children's lives. Because they feel too harried to stop and think about it, they may not realize they're actually working counter-productively. For example, a single parent who works full-time and takes on a part-time job in the evenings may be earning a relatively small monetary return for the opportunity costs incurred. Are you trading parenting opportunities for pocket change? Potential costs include:

> **No time to cook.** Increased reliance on convenience foods, which tend to be more expensive but less nutritious. Poor nutrition can lead to deterioration of health, resulting in higher medical costs.

> **Missing out on prime family time.** Dinner, bath, and bedtime rituals are key chances to connect with your children.

> **Absence from school functions.** School-age children spend most of their waking hours at school, far more hours

The assumption that someone who makes more than you do is in better financial shape than you is often incorrect.
—GINGER APPLEGARTH, THE MONEY DIET

than they spend with you. Your participation signals an interest in what goes on in their lives and keeps them motivated to succeed.

If you want to provide for your children, you must earn a certain amount of income. However, you must realize that at a certain point, the amount of that income doesn't have a direct bearing on the quality of your life. Learning how to live within your means (see Chapter 7 for tips) will serve you whether your income is $25,000 or $125,000. Move your emphasis there first, and continue to reap the benefits when you increase your income later.

Reentering the Workforce

Many single parents are unemployed because they were stay-at-home parents when they became widowed or divorced, had lost their job because of poor health or disability, were laid off, or were simply unable to find a job in the first place. For whatever reasons, the longer you are out of the workforce, the more difficult reentry can seem.

While your financial crunch may make it important to find a job—any job—to tide you over, you still need to think carefully about your long term fulfillment as well. In the short term, you may find yourself seeking help from local employment agencies (see employment in the Yellow Pages), which can place you in temporary or permanent positions. For long term change think about going back to school (more in Chapter 12) or career counseling.

Temporary help is a growing industry that already employs about 1.6 million people. You'll find wages through temporary help agencies about 15-20 percent lower than salaries for similar permanent positions. And benefits—such as the health insurance that is crucial to single parents—are typically nil. However, many take the plunge knowing that there's a chance one of their placements will lead to a permanent position. In fact, about 30 percent actually do.

Some employment agencies place you in permanent positions and generally take a percentage of your first year's salary as their payment.

Start your job search with a soul-search. Classics such as Richard Bolles' *What Color is Your Parachute? A Practical Manual for Job Hunters &*

Career Changers and Marsha Sinetar's *Do What You Love and the Money Will Follow* can help guide you to a career path that is both personally meaningful and economically feasible. Assemble a resume early in the process to help get you in touch with what you've done and the skills you've gained. As you're doing it, carefully consider what you enjoyed or disliked about particular jobs to find clues about where to go next with your career.

Working Smarter

Don't assume that you must work more to earn more. Instead, look at ways to work smarter; raising the returns for hours you already put in. The same principle applies to supplementary income, when the trade-offs mentioned earlier make your time even more valuable. Ways to work smarter include the following:

Be a valued employee. This simple piece of common sense applies to every working and earning situation. You may be biding your time waiting for something better, but don't think of it as a dead-end job or it will become one. Employers value consistent performance, creativity in problem solving, and positive attitudes. Develop these traits, and when it's time for a raise, promotion, or recommendation, your record will speak for itself. Another payoff is the increased sense of self-worth you get from a job well done.

Let your attitude work for you; not against you. Don't wait until something better comes along to start enjoying yourself. Change your attitude now, and your positive outlook will become a self-fulfilling prophecy.

Count commuting time when figuring your hourly wage. For example, if you make a $10 hourly wage, your full-time salary is $400 weekly. If you have a daily round-trip commute of two hours, you've added 10 hours to your workweek. Dividing that $400 by the actual 50 hours in your workweek gives you only an $8 hourly wage. You might as well have taken the $8 per hour job a couple of blocks down the street and walked to work. In addition to the exercise benefits, you'd have earned $320 weekly plus the chance to spend 10 hours with your kids, take a night course, or start a cottage industry in your home. Appearances can be deceiving. In this example, it appears that you'd earn $80 less per week. But savings on gas, childcare, and quality of life would offset a good deal of the decrease in earnings.

Consider working at home. If the aforementioned example appealed to you, you may be a perfect work-at-home candidate. For some, working at home means telecommuting to their current job and visiting the office for meetings or to pick up work. Other models range from a complete full-time entrepreneurial home-based business to part-time cottage industries used to supplement income. And there's the charm of working at home, the flexibility in childcare, work hours, and commuting times.

Use creative scheduling in your traditional job. Ask your employer about flextime, which would allow you to arrive or depart at varying times or days. A 40-hour work week can be achieved, for example, by working four ten-hour days or by working the traditional five days with some days being shorter or longer depending on your needs that particular day.

Think carefully about fringe benefits. Many people stay in otherwise unrewarding jobs because of health insurance benefits. Look into alternative sources of coverage. (More in Chapter 11.) Group rates are available for college students, members of national organizations such as the American Association of Working Women, and credit unions. A job with a seemingly low wage may offer hidden benefits such as profit sharing and bonus programs. Or benefits that sound great and reel you into a job may not be right for your situation anyway.

Don't be afraid to ask for a raise. Think out your points of why your work is valuable to the company. Focus on the extra hours you work, how your productivity has saved (or made) the company money. Before you ask, see two good negotiating books: Robert Mayer's *Power Plays* and the Harvard Negotiation Project's *Getting to Yes.*

Supplementing Your Income

The Work Smarter principles apply to every aspect of your income-earning life. If you must supplement your income, make sure you're doing it in a way that has the lowest opportunity costs. You may find that your source of supplemental income provides an opportunity to explore a new career path. If you can't put your finger on exactly what you want to do, consult Rebecca Maddox's *Inc. Your Dreams* for exercises that will lead you in the right direction and help you evaluate whether striking out on your own is right for you. Otherwise, consider these common ways to increase your income:

WORK AT HOME RESOURCES

Emily Card and Adam Miller. *Business Capital for Women: An Essential Handbook for Entrepreneurs.* New York: Macmillan, 1996.

Robert Mayer. *Power Plays: How to Negotiate, Persuade, and Finesse Your Way to Success in Any Situation.* New York: Times Books, 1996.

Linda Pinson and Jerry Jinnett. *The Home-Based Entrepreneur: The Complete Guide to Working at Home,* 2nd ed. New York: Upstart Publishing, 1993.

SBA Resource Directory for Small Business Management (Small Business Answer Desk 1-800-827-5722).

Internal Revenue Service: 1-800-829-FORM for free publications such as Tax Guide for Small Business (No. 334), Business Use of Your Home (No. 587), and Self-Employment Tax (No. 533).

National Association for the Self-Employed (NASE)
P.O. Box 612067
Dallas, TX 75261-2067
1-800-232-NASE (6273)

The Internet provides invaluable help for anyone working at home. Start by getting a modem and a local Internet "server" or telephone service that offers you a connection to the Internet. For the computer literate, a flat-rate service with unlimited free use and a toll-free number is most economical. You'll also need a Web browser such as Netscape or Microsoft's Windows 95 version. If you don't know computers, use a packaged service that costs more and charges by the hour but provides you with easy use.

You can search government regulations, publications, patents, and almost anything you need on the World Wide Web or the Internet.

Visit the authors at http://www.womenmoney.com where we can answer specific questions.

Many single parents feel they must take on a **part-time job** to make ends meet. Pros include flexible hours and the ability to leave work behind you when you clock out for the day. Part-time work usually requires a minimum investment of time or money to get started. On the flip side, you have to answer to someone else, the pay is minimal, and there's little or no long-term gain for your time investment. For more meaningful use of your earning time, look into other opportunities.

Network marketing, or selling by word of mouth rather than by advertising, is one way to work part-time but to retain more control over your own schedule. We all know someone who sells Mary Kay, Tupperware, Amway, Avon, or Excel. What we might not realize is that some economists see this type of direct distribution as the wave of the future. Economist Paul Zane Pilzer states that increased technology has made direct distribution the more cost-effective, leading to an industry wide growth rate that surpasses that of traditional and discount department stores. What does this mean for you? As an independent agent for a reputable direct-marketing organization, your income will relate directly to the amount of work you put in. Although you have the flexibility and freedom of being in your own business, the parent company will have guidelines to help you achieve success. After all, if you're a success, then they will be too.

The product diversity these companies offer insures that you'll find one to fit your personality. For example, if childcare is a problem, you might choose Discovery Toys and let your child tag along to the sales parties to demonstrate the toys. If you're interested in direct sales, you should write to the Direct Selling Association for its membership list that includes information on each company's products, whether it sells by parties or person to person, and what the start-up investment is. Although the members are screened, the association also offers brochures on evaluating whether a business will cost you money or make you money, codes of ethics, and how to avoid pyramid schemes.

Direct Selling Association, 1666 K Street NW Suite 1010, Washington, D.C. 20006 (202)-293-5760.

If you love **cooking,** opportunities range from baking bread on consignment for a local health food store to running a small catering business for special occasions. Even Debbi Fields of Mrs. Fields cookies got her start baking cookies from her home. Studies show that

Mary Kay Cosmetics is the only woman founded company in the Fortune 500.

Americans are eating an increasing number of meals away from home, yet there's a growing demand for healthier options. One idea: Form an entree service for several families. For a weekly subscription fee, deliver a rotating menu of fully cooked meals Monday through Thursday. Offer vegetarian or nonvegetarian plans. Check your local public health and safety regulations before getting started on any cooking enterprise.

Teaching others can be very fulfilling and often lucrative. If you have special skills or expertise, you may offer **tutoring** through libraries and local schools. Check the yellow pages for tutorial referral services to sign up with. They will screen you and refer clients to you for a cut of your hourly wage, and they typically charge a higher rate than you could get on your own. Many public libraries have a parent-teacher shelf with tutoring books to get you started.

If you're an expert or a professional, you might try **consulting** or **lecturing.** Increasingly, speakers are needed at seminars, church support groups, and library workshops. Corporations are turning to consultants for objective advice in specialized areas.

Teach a noncredit class in the Continuing Education Department of your local university, where everything from aerobics to origami (oriental paper folding) to foreign languages is offered. Typically, the Continuing Education Department will give you guidelines that help you in developing your syllabus, tell you whether your class will be on or off campus, and tell you what the charges will be. The school will publish your class in its catalog and pay you a percentage of the money. Martha Summers works full-time as a kitchen manager but is considering quitting her day job since she began teaching bread-baking and vegetarian-cooking classes. Each two-hour class requires about an hour of preparation but nets her about $150, or $50 per hour.

Computer services such as typing, word processing, and graphic design are always in demand. If you have the equipment, it's the perfect work-at-home setup. Advertise on library and campus bulletin boards. Decide if you will charge by the hour, page, or project.

For the steady-handed person, take a **calligraphy** course and earn extra dollars addressing wedding invitations and school diplomas.

Advertise at bridal shops, contact local schools and universities, and post fliers (with handwriting samples, of course!) on bulletin boards around town.

Dreaming of making money by writing? While this is not a traditionally lucrative field, certain writing skills are much in demand. **Grant writing** (helping organizations apply for grants) pays surprisingly well. After all, a successful grant request can mean thousands for the organization.

And then there are those individuals who find a niche **creating a product.** Ideas include growing herbs for specialty restaurants and grocery stores, gift baskets, and arts and crafts. The possibilities are as varied as your imagination.

Special Projects is the category reserved as a catchall for one-shot deals or periodic events. For example, one father sold Christmas trees for three years in a row, netting a profit of more than $25,000, which he used to buy a house. On a smaller scale, weekend garage sales can pad your pockets with a little extra cash while helping you slough off some of those possessions that are weighing you down. A slightly more sophisticated version of the yard sale is a consignment sale, where goods are collected from a number of people and the person holding the sale gets a set percentage. Ginia Scott makes an extra 3 to 4 thousand dollars annually by holding two such sales, or what amounts to a couple of well-organized weeks of work per year.

Before plunging into any money-making endeavor, ask yourself why you're seeking supplemental income. Are you starting a sideline business in hopes of breaking away from your regular job? Do you have a certain goal in mind, such as just making enough to save for your child's education? Or are you doing this out of desperation because you just can't seem to make ends meet? If you know why you're doing it and what it's for but you can't decide exactly what to do, evaluate your options with the following questions: What investments of time and money would be required? What is the potential payoff and profit? Does it require any further training? Which "Work Smarter" principles apply? And finally, is it something I enjoy? After all, your sideline business may grow into a fulfilling career.

LIFESTYLE CHOICES

Ideally, we'd all spend equal time each day on rest, work, and play. In the real world, the scales are dramatically tipped in the direction of work, which gobbles up more and more of our rest and playtime. In fact, if we divided each 24-hour day into thirds, we'd get about 8 hours to work (when we're at our job and our kids are at school), 8 hours of sleep (well, we hope our kids are getting that much, anyway), and 8 hours to play, right? You know the answer is wrong because that last 8 hours must also be used for homework, housework, our physical needs for food and cleanliness, and perhaps even a part-time job to boot. Running the numbers shows us that we must carefully exercise our choices to squeeze the most out of every experience and avoid the "all-work-no-play-makes-parents-crash-and-burn" syndrome.

Who says work, play, and rest can't overlap? In the aforementioned example of an average workday, the most time you could possibly spend with your children would be 8 hours. But one study showed that parents actually spend only 6 minutes a day in face-to-face conversation with their children. Out of 1,440 minutes in a day! How can you increase the precious time you spend with your children and remain financially solvent? If feasible for you, take your children on business trips and occasional regular workdays. Turn off the TV and eat dinner with your child. Even a frozen dinner becomes special when eaten by candlelight in the company of your loved ones. Use your new time awareness as motivation to stick to your financial goals. Lifestyle choices boil down to the choices we make each moment that affect our future.

Time-busters: Licking Your Top Culprits

Time is all we really have. You've heard it before and you'll hear it again. But what does it really mean? Top executives think of time as money. If they're making a certain salary, they can easily figure what their time is worth in dollars down to the minute. So they know, for instance, that five minutes spent listening to an annoying telemarketer is $5.60 down the drain. That analogy is crucial for many people, and it's a helpful reminder even for those of us who realize that time is far more valuable than money. So how can you keep from wasting it? We all have our weaknesses. Perhaps you'll find yours here.

Time-buster 1: Telephones. In the age of communications, telephones are a necessity for business, education, and feeling connected to those we love. They are also annoyances, interruptions, and major culprits in the losing battle with time. People who would never dream of wasting their employer's time by gabbing away at work don't think twice about wasting their own time at home.

Working at home is a true telephone dilemma. Friends often assume that it's okay to call you; telemarketers find out they can target you, and all of a sudden, you're missing important business calls.

Time-buster 2: Paperwork. It seems like running a household has gotten more and more complicated. We must comb through piles of mail, shuffle around increasingly larger piles of paperwork, and keep the systems running smoothly. My mother's monthly ledger from the 1940s might have had entries such as groceries, clothing, and gasoline, paid for mostly with cash and the occasional check. Monthly notes for a house and utilities were the major expenses. Modern heads of households juggle an average of six credit cards and write more than 50 checks per month. Their fixed expenses might include student loan payments, car notes, and insurance premiums in addition to my mother's simple house and utilities payments; dramatically increasing the paperwork by sheer volume.

Time-buster 3: Interruptions from your children. Don't get me wrong. I know you want more free time with them. But anyone who has cared for a newborn knows that it takes four or five times longer to do anything when your children are around. (Remember the early weeks when your big accomplishment for the day was to take a shower and by then it was time to cook dinner?) Simply getting in and out of a car with your child can take up to 15 minutes. And that's before you've even left the driveway. Unfortunately, it doesn't really get easier; just different as their needs change.

As with physical health, prevention is the best medicine for children who crave your loving attention as much as their next meal. When

TELEPHONE GUIDELINES

Put yourself in the driver's seat. By screening your calls with an answering machine or caller ID, you choose whom you want to speak with and when.

Don't be a slave to a ringing telephone. Although they may feel absolutely compelled to answer the phone, many people are afraid to turn off the ringer for fear of missing emergency calls from family, friends, or caretakers. Again, use technology. If you don't want to turn off the ringer, subscribe to a ringmaster service and assign a different number to key people. Or get a beeper instead.

Put your E-mail address and/or fax number on your answering machine. Doing so encourages callers to contact you in a written format, which you can process at your convenience.

Be proactive with telemarketers. Sure they have a tough job, but if you're not going to buy anything, you shouldn't waste their time and yours by politely listening to their spiel and then turning them down. New federal legislation against abusive telemarketers is on your side. Any company that calls you back even once after you've asked them not to is in violation, and you should report such a company to your state attorney general's office.

children are clingy and pester you constantly (my mother called this behavior "chunking"), they are actually so desperate for attention that they're willing to do anything to get it; even if it turns out to be a negative interaction. In other words, you're tired, the kid's tired, the kid drives you crazy, and you yell at him. Your defense? Cut off your children at the pass by doling out your loving attention before they think they need it. Twenty minutes of quality time at key points in the day (such as when you first return from work) can save you an entire evening of interruptions, hassles, and drained energy. The child will get the attention either way, so you might as well give it sooner and willingly rather than later and grudgingly. You both will win.

Time-buster 4: Household Maintenance. Unfortunately, one less parent theoretically equals twice as much work for you (unless your spouse was a high maintenance person). While helpful friends and relatives may buzz around at first, mowing your yard or folding your laundry, the day will come when the entire weight of domestic routines will fall on you. Consider hiring help. If you think you can't afford it, consider this: Now more than ever, your time is precious, and you're going to spread yourself too thin if you attempt to do it all. Rethinking your routines may help. One mother found that she could afford hiring a housekeepre if she reduced the hours her daughter was in day care. Because she was freed from her household chores, she could spend more time with her daughter. Result: quality time with her daughter, burden lifted from her shoulders.

Whether or not you're able to hire help, you can save time and concern over household chores by following our three Ds: **Delegate** to your children when appropriate; **Daily** maintenance on each room; and **Deep** clean only when needed.

Delegate: Even a two-year-old is capable of putting toys in a toy box or on a shelf. Four-year-olds can set and clear the dinner table, 8-year-olds can take out the trash or run a simple load of laundry, and 16-year-olds can mow the yard or wash the car. Be creative and teach personal responsibility at a young age.

Daily maintenance: Spend five to ten minutes making a quick sweep of each room. Set a timer and play race the clock; you'll surprise yourself at how much you can get done. If you do it before you leave in the morning, you'll be greeted with a clutter-free home when you return from work.

Deep cleaning: Tasks that take larger chunks of time, such as mopping, cleaning the refrigerator, or washing your bed linens, can be saved for the weekend or for the housekeeper, depending on your circumstances.

In general, clean areas that will be seen first. A guest who sees your tidy entry and living room has no way of knowing that your bedroom is a mess. Perhaps more importantly, it's the first thing YOU see when you come home from your tough day to face a night alone with your kids.

Time-buster 5: Errands. Now here's where your frame of mind really affects your pocketbook. Have you ever grocery shopped on an empty stomach? What happens when you take your kids along?

TRANSFORMING YOUR RELATIONSHIP WITH PAPERWORK

Create a simple **filing system** to make a place for your important papers. Your creditor doesn't want to hear that you "had the money, but the bill got shoved to the back of the drawer and I forgot about it," as one woman wrote. Use files for tax-related receipts; each major company, creditor, or bank account; a general file for subscriptions; unpaid bills, and letters to answer. If you like to keep mementos, you should have a file marked "memories 1995" to file your play programs, special notes from your child, newspaper clippings, and calendar pages you've written on. Each year when you do your taxes, you'll put all the paperwork from that year together in a big envelope or box with the year clearly marked and store it someplace where it won't be in the way. Memory files can go in a special file folder box all together. You may want to have one for each member of the family.

Process your **mail** like a pro. As you come to each piece, take immediate action or designate it for future action. Bills can be placed in the unpaid bills file, letters in the letters-to-answer file, and so on. Direct marketing mail should be put in a separate place and tossed periodically unless you need the product that's offered. Make a charitable giving budget rather than responding to every mail solicitation. Or choose one favorite charity to give your time or money.

Be your own **bookkeeper.** Keep regular bimonthly (such as the 1st and 15th) appointments with yourself to do your paperwork. Take these sessions seriously, as if you were actually meeting someone at an office. At each appointment, think ahead about your financial needs until the next session. Note when your money is coming in and when the bills come due, as well as assessing your successes and setbacks on your budget plan.

Simplify, Simplify, Simplify. Why carry three different department store credit cards with three accompanying statements to receive, checks to write, envelopes to lick, and stamps to buy, when one Visa or Mastercard would do? Major department stores charge the maximum interest allowed in their states; yet they generally take Visas and Mastercards, which carry much more competitive interest rates. *Exception:* If you're divorced or widowed and had little or no credit in your name, be cautious about canceling accounts that were in your name.

Compare doing all errands in a planned day with doing one at a time throughout the week. Let Your Fingers Do the Walking—and the driving. Never drive when you could call. Find a dry cleaner and grocery that deliver for free. To save time, avoid taking the children unless you're teaching them an economics lesson.

Time-buster 6: Brain Candy. We all need downtime, unwind time, and time to just lose ourselves in a "fluff" activity. Predictable romance novels, old movies, or channel surfing are a few typical outlets for our unfocused energy. But with only slightly more effort we can find activities that are more rewarding than the ubiquitous television plug-in drug. See Parent Pampering in Chapter Five for more constructive ways to relax as well as the following ideas for inexpensive family entertainment.

Time-buster 7: Worry. You know that single parents have plenty to worry about. We sometimes think of worry as a sign that we care. After all, would we worry about our teenager staying out all night if we didn't love him? But worry keeps us trapped. Our nonconstructive thoughts keep circulating and we become paralyzed with fear. Worst of all are the medical implications. Worry causes stress and stress-related diseases such as ulcers.

Try thinking of your worries simply as problems to be solved. Successful problem solving results from gathering the facts, analyzing them, deciding what steps to take, and taking those steps. Too many of us jump ahead, agonizing over all the possible outcomes before we look calmly at the situation at hand. If your thoughts are running wild, tame them by focusing on the

HIRING DOMESTIC HELP

A 1995 survey reported in USA Today asked what would make respondents' lives easier. "Housekeeper or gardener" got more votes than any other single category.

Know What You Want

Before you begin your search, you should know what you're looking for. Do you want someone to come once a month and do your heavy cleaning, or would you prefer help weekly? Write out a list of duties you expect the help to accomplish. Do you expect any childcare? Would you feel comfortable leaving your child with the housekeeper while you run a quick errand? Or do you expect the maid to do your errands for you?

A Good Housekeeper Is Hard to Find

Hard, but not impossible. The best source: personal referrals. Ask your friends, other parents at your child's school or daycare, or people at the gym.

It's also worth calling real estate agents in nicer neighborhoods. If a family is moving out of town, their housekeeper may be out of a job. The agent will be glad to find out for you.

The Interview

It's essential to interview several prospects in person if you've never hired household help before. If the personality doesn't complement yours, find someone else. Skills are important, too. Go over your list of expectations. If you have an unusual job like cleaning the kitty litter box, say so now.

A must: Ask for (and check) a minimum of two references. You should also inquire whether the person is licensed and bonded although most household help isn't unless you go through a service. Never hire on the spot. Instead, promise to call within a specified time whether or not you need the services.

Compensation and Paperwork

You will set rates during the interview based on what their references pay and any special needs you have. Will you pay by the task or by the hour? Will fringe benefits be included? For instance, it is customary to give one-day-a-week workers two days of paid vacation, a sick day, and a paid holiday each year. Keep it legal by paying Social Security for any regular help that earns over $1,000 per year. You will file Schedule H, Household Employment Tax, along with your regular 1040. One way to avoid this paperwork is by going through an established service, though it may be more expensive and you won't have as much control.

moment at hand. Writing down your worries often helps you clear your mind and serves as a way to organize any actions you may need to take.

FAMILY ENTERTAINMENT FOR $10 OR LESS

- **Top pick: The public library.** From an entertainment perspective, libraries offer something for every member of the family: puppet shows, seminars, inexpensive video and CD rentals, and of course, the books.

- **Public parks:** Take a simple picnic lunch and read a good book while your kids fly a kite or throw a Frisbee.

- **"Pay what you can" days** at the symphony, theater, zoo, museums. Call and find out when local attractions offer reduced rates. Consider purchasing a family membership to your favorite spots for a year of unlimited visits and other perks. Two single parents I know teamed up to split the cost of the local zoo's family package, which allowed up to two named adults and four named children regardless of relationships.

- **Second-run movies** for about $1.50 per ticket.

- **Indoor "cookout"**: Eat hot dogs and roasted marshmallows (roast in the oven if you don't have a fireplace). Camp out on the living room floor with sleeping bags.

- **Minor league baseball games** or sporting events at your children's schools (the latter often offer free admission).

- **Watch TV—TOGETHER.** Talk about the story line during the commercials. Have your kids identify main characters and supporting characters. Discuss what makes something a comedy, drama, or suspense show. The commercials themselves can be entertaining to children. Be sure to explain that commercials are trying to sell us something. Consult *The Smart Parent's Guide to KIDS' TV* by Milton Chen, Ph.D. (San Francisco: KQED Books, 1994) for more ideas.

THE CHILDCARE DILEMMA

If you're more worried about where your child will go for day care than college, you're not alone. Finding high-quality affordable childcare is one of the toughest challenges you'll face as a single parent. In addition to normal feelings of worry or guilt for being away from your child, you have the added burden of knowing that there is really no backup. If your child is sick or if your arrangements fall apart, you must deal with the situation alone. Knowing your options from the start can help you build a safety net of contingency plans if there's trouble.

If you aren't happy with your current circumstances, use our tips for finding childcare you can afford. Although expense is not necessarily an indication of excellence, if you find an excellent situation that costs more than you wanted to spend, you shouldn't automatically rule it out. The peace of mind that you gain by knowing your child is well cared for will help motivate you to save in other areas. In general and if at all possible, you should choose an arrangement first by its suitability for your child and second by its effect on your pocketbook.

What to Look For

Childcare is not one-size-fits-all. An ideal fit considers the values and pocketbook of the parent as well as the personality and age of the child. While it's hard enough to find a fit for an only child, parents of more than one face a seemingly unconquerable financial burden and a dizzying array of scheduling conflicts. Because of differences in their ages, it's rare to find a single solution that works for all.

A good starting point for evaluating any day care is to obtain a copy of the licensing requirements for your state. However, even if a center meets the standards to a tee and comes with a shining recommendation from your friends, it may not be right for you and your child. Use your intuition before you place your child anywhere. Outside of abusive situations, there's no right and wrong about childcare. Think instead of differences in perspective. After all, a caregiver is there for most of your child's waking hours, and you hope that the person's child-rearing values and practices will match yours and complement them too.

Many parents feel safest with an accredited day care that is affiliated with a larger organization, such as national franchises or centers found in churches or universities. State accreditation is also available for home care or private day care facilities. Many parents look to full-time day

One fourth of working parents with children under age 13 have had a childcare breakdown in the past three months.
—The Families and Work Institute.

care facilities to meet their needs, enjoying the availability of longer hours (usually 7 A.M. to 6 P.M.) as well as the knowledge that the center provides backup when the child's teacher is sick.

Due to lack of programs, most single parents turn to home care situations to meet their needs. In spite of TV news magazine exposés on these caregivers, there are still plenty of honest, loving, and hardworking people that care for children in their own homes. They tend to be less expensive and to have smaller teacher-to-student ratios, and offer a comforting home environment. But they often rely on the TV rather than on educational activities and peer training. Potential problems include a lack of backup if the baby-sitter gets sick or goes on vacation, failure to meet state-licensing requirements, and an increased likelihood of abuse because there's no one around to check up on them.

Nanny services that care for your children in your home may often be overlooked because of a perception that they're more expensive. But some parents still depend on this approach. The children stay in a familiar home environment and have one-on-one interaction with their caregiver, and the parents save valuable commuting time. This option may be particularly suitable for families with more than one child because services typically charge a base rate for one child and a smaller fee for each additional child, making the per child average more manageable.

JUGGLING CHILDCARE OPTIONS

- Robert Miller works full-time and attends night school. He was lucky to find a nice home care situation for his toddler daughter, that is on his way to work. However, the preschool that his four-year-old attends is across the city, closer to grandma's house. In a pinch, grandma can pick her up in the evenings when Robert can't make it on time. In general, he feels the commute is worth it for the peace of mind of knowing that his child is well cared for, but he admits that it's difficult juggling three different schedules.
- Single parent Lisa Jones has a successful but solo dental practice. Without backup, she returned to work when her infant son was only a month old. Rather than give up nursing her child, and lacking other arrangements, she turned a spare room at the office into a nursery and hired a teenager to mind the baby while she was with patients.

BACK-UP CHILDCARE

No matter what your primary arrangements are, the odds say they'll fall through at some point or another. Prompted by the huge cost of employee absenteeism to care for children, many large companies are buying slots in special drop-in day cares that require only a 30-minute advance warning. Contact Lipton Corporate Child Care Centers, Inc. (202-416-6875) for information on such arrangements and to see if your company might be a candidate.

In addition, check into hospital "Sick-Bay" services at local hospitals. Some hospitals offer a special room or unit for sick child day care. It may be more expensive, but worth it for emergencies when you simply must get to work. Don't wait until your child is sick. Call now and find out if you must preregister and request an information packet.

If an in home worker sounds good to you but you desire more peer interaction for your children, require the nanny to take your children to regular play groups. Send a SASE to the American Council of Nanny Schools for a list of schools that provide placement services. A-74 Delta College, University Center, Michigan 48710; (517) 686-9417.

Creative Options

Single parents often need to think more creatively about their childcare options simply because time and money are tight. If you have more than one child, you're probably looking at finding more than one situation to meet the needs of different age groups. Beyond the statistics, many parents are piecing together a patchwork of childcare options to make a system that's not always user-friendly work for them.

For the right family, an au pair, or caretaker from another country who lives with you as a member of the family, could be the answer. Considering that parents spend upwards of $500 per month for full time day care, or $6,000 annually *per child* (the national median is $388 a month per child but it is much higher in metro areas), the expenses of hiring an au pair could well be justified. If there are several children, the single parent would potentially save money as well as benefit from the extra pair of hands. The children would benefit from exposure to another culture. Also, consider hiring a domestic (U.S. citizen) au pair for summer help when your kids are out of school. Call the U.S. Information Agency at (202) 401-9810, for regulations governing au pairs and a list of au pair agencies that meet the regulations.

If you yearn to be a stay-at-home parent or feel that you're working just to pay the childcare bills, consider making your children (and other people's children) your work. After all, you kill two birds with one stone: You save money on your own day care and commuting costs, and you make money filling a big need. However, if you're the type of person that likes to drop everything and get the hell out of Dodge, this job isn't for you. The trade-off for spending your days with your children is little vacation time and little or no flexibility in your schedule. It helps to form a network with other home providers, avoiding feelings of isolation while serving as backup for one another in case of illness, emergencies, or vacations. Don't fool yourself with romantic notions; running a home day care is not child's play. To succeed, you must run it like the business that it is. Look to your state's laws as well as the many excellent guidebooks available for help in getting started.

Getting childcare help from relatives can be a mixed blessing. Even when they're paid, it's likely to be much harder for you to make demands about the way they treat your child. After all, "they raised you and you turned out fine, didn't you?" It helps to have a thorough understanding in the first place, so they don't feel taken advantage of and you don't feel like you're stepping on their toes. Turning to family doesn't have to be a permanent solution either. It may be necessary when your children are younger and space is either nonexistent or extremely expensive or when you're in transition and making other arrangements.

THE NIGHT SHIFT

Parents working non-traditional hours sometimes resort to desperate measures. One factory-working mother would bundle up her sleeping children and leave them in her car while she worked the night shift. Others piece together haphazard arrangements, with children sleeping at the homes of friends and relatives. 24-hour learning centers are springing up around the country to meet the need.

The quilted approach: You work nontraditional hours, your income doesn't justify paying for full-time day care, or you just can't find a suitable full-time position. You improvise. Patch together a network of providers and wing it on a weekly or even daily basis. Thousands of other single parents do it. If the noncustodial parent works a different schedule, you may be able to spot each other for some hours. Tap into relatives and friends; paying with swapped baby-sitting time or insisting on giving them something in return (after all, they're likely to be closing in on burnout too). Don't overlook extended care before and after school, summer camps, day camps, and big brother and big sister programs. Check local universities for early childhood education majors to help you either by watching your children or by picking them up from school. Start a baby-sitting co-op; although this implies that you have time to devote to it. Perhaps you could trade other services such as carpool duty for another parent's baby-sitting help. Avoid children home alone if you can, but by preteen years an hour or two at home may be a time to learn indepence.

Survey all your options before making a choice. If your child is in an adequate situation, think of it as a "holding pattern" while you gather more information about other possibilities. In general, children thrive on the stability of the same familiar setting and routine every day, but this may not be the solution that works best for you. What if you can't find an appropriate or affordable day care? Or what if you find one but have to get on a waiting list? You must go to the next best option for the moment but by all means keep working on it until you find a situation you're absolutely comfortable with. You may even find that your temporary arrangements were the best bet in the first place.

RESOURCES

Joan Anderson. *The Single Mother's Book.* Atlanta: Peachtree Publishers, Ltd., 1990.

Ginger Applegarth. *The Money Diet.* New York: Viking, 1995.

If you pay your in-home caretaker more than $1,000 per year, you must pay Social Security and Medicaid taxes. You must also withdraw federal (and sometimes state) unemployment taxes. Call the IRS publication order line (800-829-3676) to request publication #926, Household Employees Tax. Call the IRS TeleTax line (800-829-4477) to listen to taped messages on this and other topics.

If you are lucky enough to have relatives to help with baby-sitting, treat them like solid gold.

—JOAN ANDERSON, THE SINGLE MOTHER'S BOOK

TIPS FOR PARENTS OF CHILDREN HOME ALONE

1. Make sure your child calls you at work as soon as he or she arrives home.

2. Post a list of emergency numbers and go over them with your child. Include the usual police, ambulance, doctor, and fire department as well as a number where you can be reached and the number of an adult friend.

3. Teach safety rules such as "stop, drop, and roll" if your clothing catches fire, be on the lookout for unusual circumstances when first arriving home and immediately leave if an intruder is suspected, and never alert callers that there's no one else home.

4. Leave a signed and notarized authorization form for emergency medical treatment. Show your child the first aid kit and how to use it.

5. Importantly, set strict guidelines for your child about activities you will or won't allow, whether friends may visit, whether appliances may be used, and what time to arrive home.

As a rule, the younger the child, the less available are day care spaces. Because care is so labor intensive, spaces that are available may be as much as 20 percent more expensive.

Richard Bolles. *What Color is Your Parachute? A Practical Manual for Job Hunters and Career Changers.* Berkeley, CA: Ten Speed Press, 1996.

Emily Card and Adam Miller. *Business Capital for Women: An Essential Handbook for Entrepreneurs.* New York: Macmillan, 1996.

Dale Carnegie. *How to Stop Worrying and Start Living.* New York: Simon & Schuster, 1984.

Milton Chen, Ph.D. *The Smart Parent's Guide to KIDS' TV.* San Francisco: KQED Books, 1994.

Joline Godfrey. *No More Frogs to Kiss: 99 Ways to Give Economic Power to Girls.* New York: HarperCollins, 1995

Joline Godfrey. *Our Wildest Dreams: Women Entrepreneurs Making Money, Doing Good, Having Fun.* New York: HarperCollins, 1993.

Steffan T. Kraehmer. *Quantity Time: Moving Beyond the Quality Time Myth.* Minneapolis: Deaconess Press, 1994.

Diane Lusk and Bruce McPherson. *Nothing But the Best: Making Day Care Work for You and Your Child*. New York: William Morrow & Co., 1992.

Rebecca Maddox. *Inc. Your Dreams*. NY: Viking, 1995.

Robert Mayer. *Power Plays: How to Negotiate, Persuade, and Finesse Your Way to Success in any Situation*. New York: Time Books, 1996.

Linda Pinson and Jerry Jinnett. *The Home-Based Entrepreneur: The Complete Guide to Working at Home*. Second Edition New York: Upstart Publishing, 1993.

Nancy Schumann and William Lewis. *Back to Work: How to Re-Enter the Working World*. Woodbury, NY: Barron's, 1985.

Martha Sinetar. *Do What You Love and the Money Will Follow*. New York: Dell Publishers, 1989.

Evonne Weinhaus and Karen Friedman. *Stop Struggling with Your Child*. New York: HarpersCollins, 1991.

CHAPTER 7

Let's Make a Deal—Living on Less

One of the hardest lessons I had to learn as a single parent was that, inevitably, I was living with more to do and less time to do it. The second hardest? Sooner or later, compromises happen. The single parent who doesn't make adjustments is on a collision course with financial disaster.

Taking time to find good deals can be a tough adjustment if your previous lifestyle was less restrictive. I've found that it's important to balance the cost of my time versus savings on smaller items. In general, "don't sweat the small stuff" is my motto, although my friends call me "The Queen of Takeback." If something doesn't work, I'm "in their face" with my hand out for a refund. You'll find your own cost-cutting pleasures.

This chapter walks you through the delights and downfalls of living on less. After all, if you see it as a fun challenge on the good days, the bad days won't seem so hard. First, we'll start with a general examination of your spending habits and ways to change. Then, we'll get a little more specific with techniques for downsizing and streamlining major areas of your life such as food, clothing, shelter, transportation, and yes, your children's toys. Finally, the chapter closes with specific negotiating and money-saving strategies that will help you get more bang for your buck and satisfaction as a consumer. Along the way you'll find ways to break free of the consumer mind-set trap and tips on rating the effectiveness of your cost-cutting measures.

ADJUSTING YOUR SPENDING STYLE

The impact of your everyday expenses can't be overemphasized. When I say "don't sweat the small stuff," I mean "don't let the details bog you down." But part of your balancing act is your giving enough attention to the details, so that your financial bottom line remains in order. Sounds like conflicting advice, but it's not. In "Budget Basics" you saw how to build a little leeway into your budget for cash expenses. Here, we'll explore your spending personality and help you adjust it to your financial reality

Old Habits Die Hard

When faced with a new financial reality, many balk, using credit cards or floating checks to maintain the status quo at all costs. One single mother said, "I've been getting my weekly facial for so long that I simply can't do without it." But with creditors hounding her and at the thought of losing her home, she was able to find the motivation to change. Her challenge is now to maintain the change even after the initial threats are gone. That's the challenge for all of us who start with the best of intentions, see our enthusiasm peak as we see the results of our first big changes, then fall back on old habits when we think we've hit easy street. For lasting change, take it slow and easy. Learn where changes will make the biggest difference and concentrate on those areas first. And don't beat up on yourself when you don't meet you're goals. Find the lesson from your setback and move on.

DOWNSIZING

Also known as "trimming the fat," downsizing is a corporate term for cutting costs. In many people's minds, the term has become synonymous with thoughts of layoffs, management restructuring, and slashed budgets. On the home front, single parents faced with slashed budgets of their own may choose to downsize now or be forced to do it later.

This strategy will work for you if you use it with the other strategies. If you see downsizing as a permanent measure, you may feel deprived.

The average consumer carries a $3,000 balance on credit cards.

If you see it in the context of obtaining your overall financial goals, you'll feel empowered and satisfied. You have to find a balance between looking forward to your goals and enjoying the moment. An ancient parable tells of a soldier marching toward a distant mountain. If his sole focus is the distant horizon, he will stumble over the rough terrain. Yet if he looks only at the ground below his feet, he may lose sight of his destination and take a wrong turn. To arrive safely, he must strike a balance between the distant horizon and the momentary details of the terrain. Your financial planning is like the soldier's distant horizon; the task of downsizing is just one of the brambles in your path.

Guiding Principles

Successful downsizing occurs when you learn to use the least that is appropriate in any given situation. To attain this general goal, make use of the two supporting principles: Change your thinking, and streamline your systems.

First, change your thinking. A tendency in our consumer-oriented society is to equate more material goods with feelings of prosperity and wealth. Ironically, if we obtain these items by overextending ourselves, we will go another way entirely: bankruptcy or insolvency. Keeping up with the Joneses is really just keeping yourself stuck in a vicious spend cycle. Do yourself a favor and don't do it. Change your expectations to match your financial reality at the moment. But don't fall into the limiting trap of thinking life will always be this way. Remember, you're choosing to be proactive now to ensure your security later.

As your thinking changes, you'll recognize the value of streamlining your systems. Streamlining means deciding what absolutely must be done and then finding a way to do it as efficiently as possible. Start with the basics of food, clothing, and shelter. Downsizing can apply to all aspects of your life. Use these ideas as a starting point in your quest for a simpler lifestyle.

Food

Acquisition, preparation, and consumption of food are basic to our survival. Yet most of us are largely unconscious of our food choices; basing them on habits or media hype rather than on a coordinated system. Streamlining here often affects your waist as well as your wallet, since processed food is more expensive and less nutritious.

If cooking is not your forte, you probably spend more on food. Most of the price of restaurant food is labor. You're paying someone else to cook, serve, and clean up for you. Depending on your finances, what you used to take for granted may now become a special occasion treat. Make the most out of your restaurant dollars:

THE PANTRY PRINCIPLE: SAVING YOUR FOOD DOLLARS

From toilet tissue to tuna fish you should *never wait until you've run out of anything before purchasing more.* Start with an initial investment of completely stocking your pantry with the basics. Keep a running list on your pantry or refrigerator door when you use the NEXT to the last of any item. Follow up with a weekly shopping trip to replace what you used that week and to add fresh produce and perishables for next week.

Order lower on the food chain—vegetarian entrees are often less expensive than meat dishes.

Let appetizers serve as main course—mini pizzas, antipastos, or nachos can actually give you a balanced meal. Cheese and crackers and fruit trays are great finger foods for young children.

Drink water—Request a lemon wedge to give it more pizzazz. If you must order a beverage, get one that comes with free refills.

Skip dessert or split it with your kids.

Don't eat everything on your plate. Eat half and have the server put the rest in a "to go" container. Violá—tomorrow's lunch or tonight's midnight snack.

Go to an all-you-can-eat buffet if you and the kids are really hungry.

Don't skimp on the tip. Next time you're in alone with your child, you'll be welcomed and given good service if you frequent the same establishments and give good tips.

REALITY CHECK MENU PLANNING

If you're like most single parents, tonight's dinner looks more like a Hamburger Helper commercial than a Martha Stewart masterpiece. Few of us have time to orchestrate complicated home-cooked meals. But taking a few minutes each week to plan ahead will cut down on the poor food decisions we make when our stomachs are grumbling, saving time and money in the end.

- Take the pain out of menu planning by assigning a theme for each night of the week. If Monday is your toughest night, make it "convenience" night by eating takeout, frozen dinners, or even Sunday's leftovers. If your children are older, assign them a night to be responsible for the meal. (Most kids could put together simple sandwiches, hot dogs, and baked French fries, etc.)

- Other useful categories include pasta, soup and sandwich and salad, one-dish meal, vegetarian, meat and potatoes, and international. The point here is to save time by limiting choices.

- Beware of the "what's-for-dinner" blues. If you leave the house undecided, it'll only hang over you all day and remain unresolved by the time you pick up your hungry children from the baby-sitter, and you'll end up in line at the McDonalds drive-through.

- Cyclical sales will help you keep in touch with the yearly seasons as well as keep your food costs down. Seasonal produce costs less and peaks in flavor and nutrition. Request a calendar of seasonal produce from your agricultural extension service (even metropolitan areas have these nearby; check in the Government Blue Pages of your telephone book). Other cycles hinge around holidays, both secular and spiritual. Thus, purchase your year's worth of baking supplies at Thanksgiving, or get the cheapest prices on eggs at Easter.

After eating out, the next most expensive food choice is home delivery or takeout. Depending on your local options, this category may actually be a good solution for the busy single parent on a particularly hectic evening. Keep a folder of menus handy at home or at the office and consider calling ahead before you leave work to avoid the wait.

Our nation's reliance on convenience foods has been blamed for many of our health concerns and the growing costs of our food dollar.

But like takeout, convenience foods can be a good choice when used with discretion. It's increasingly possible to strike a balance between time, expense, and nutrition.

Even if you don't like to cook, you should use the pantry principle to keep your shelves well stocked. It will help you break the vicious cycle of "just picking up a few groceries on the way home from work." After all, who enjoys battling other harried shoppers for parking spaces and a place in the checkout lanes with their hungry kids in tow? Whether you're living on an earthquake fault, hurricane zone, or tornado corridor (or all of the above like the authors), it's smart to keep nonperishables handy for emergencies. And best of all, you'll save money. When you flip on the TV to watch the evening news and a pizza commercial gets you salivating, your self-control will be bolstered if you know you've got a delicious frozen lasagna ready to pop in the oven and salad fixings in the fridge.

Frozen vegetables may seem more expensive than canned, but they actually retain more of their vitamins and minerals, making them a better overall value.

Take advantage of "loss leaders" and cyclical sales to stock up on pantry basics. Loss leaders are the items the stores sell below cost to get you into the food store, knowing that you'll probably go ahead and buy all your groceries because you're already there. But there's nothing wrong with just buying the loss leaders. If you know your family uses about a can of tuna each week, buy 52 cans when they're 39 cents each. You won't have to worry about tuna for a whole year, and you'll save 61 cents a can, or about $32. This may not sound like much, but it represents more than a 60 percent return on your "investment" in pre-tax dollars.

Clothes

Think of clothes as an investment, right? Wrong. Anything that depreciates in value from the time you buy it is not an investment.

Don't use this common rationalization for spending too much on clothes. Instead, change your thinking and place an emphasis on the quality rather than on the quantity of your own and your children's wardrobes. Streamline your clothing needs by building a core wardrobe of quality basics, by learning where to get the best deals on clothes, and finally, by taking proper care of them to make them last longer.

Goodwill Industries has reported over 11 percent growth for two years running, with over $500 million in revenues for 1995.

Every woman knows the value of the "little black dress" that can be worn to practically every occasion. Men, too, can get away with a minimum of suits by simply changing shirts and ties. Evaluate each clothing purchase with the following questions: Do I feel comfortable wearing it (in a literal and personality sense)? Does it have quality construction? (Check buttons, seams, material.) Is it a classic style? What do I already have that matches it? If it's a sale item, do I like it so much I would have paid full price for it? (This one's a clincher because we often get lured into purchasing clothes we'll never wear because "it's such a good deal.") Does the price fit my budgeted amount for clothing expenses? And

LAUNDRY 101

The initial purchase price of a garment is only a portion of the total amount you spend over the life of that garment. Streamlining your laundry systems will save you time, money, water, and energy while preventing pollution as well.

Use dry cleaners judiciously. Many states are passing environmental legislation that will affect your pocketbook in two ways. First, clean-up efforts where decades-old underground storage tanks have seeped toxic chemicals will be funded in part by taxpayer money. Second, the costs of heavy taxes on perchlorethelene, an essential dry-cleaning chemical that can contaminate groundwater, will be passed along in higher bills for the consumer.

Hand-wash Instead. Most "dry cleaning preferred" and some "dry clean only" garments can safely be hand-washed in cold water and line-dried. You are safest when the natural fabrics such as cotton, linen, and wool are less than 100 percent of the fabric content.

Use less detergent and buy scent-free ecologically sound detergent in bulk. Much of the detergent we use is overkill; in fact, after washing in recommended amounts of a major brand, there's enough detergent residue to wash again.

Save time: Delegate to your children. Learning how to sort, choose correct settings, fold, and put away laundry can teach children personal responsibility as well as take a load off your back.

finally, what are the hidden care costs? (Dry cleaning only, hand washing, and ironing are time and money hogs.)

For deals on clothes, try your luck at thrift stores and charity auctions. Auctions are the hottest new way for organizations, churches, or even your child's school to raise money, as members donate items which are auctioned to the highest bidder. From new clothing with the tags still attached to unopened gift-quality books, you're sure to find a buried treasure.

Another favorite is the factory outlet store. For shoes and clothing, the prices can be fabulous. As I travel a lot on business, I have found the local specialties and try to take advantage when I'm in town. When business takes me to Georgia, for example, I find textiles such as curtains, sheets, or rugs and have them shipped home. Find out if you have a factory outlet mall within driving distance. Though the prices are higher than, say, the thrift stores or garage sales, time-conscious folks will appreciate the convenience of one-stop shopping and prices well below retail.

FACT:

Children's feet can grow as much as 2$\frac{1}{2}$ sizes per year.

Shelter

While the divorced parent may have received a house in the settlement, many single parents find themselves relocating. Remember, landlords are looking for the most reliable applicants. If you have a good track record as a renter, you should be able to negotiate the rent and deposits. Ask your potential landlord to take half the deposit now and to spread the rest over the next few months. Or if the landlord won't reduce the rent permanently, you may be able to negotiate by starting lower and gradually increasing over the first year while you get back on your feet.

In living space, less can be more. The financial benefits of streamlining your space include the following: smaller places generally cost less whether you're renting or buying; utilities will be lower; fewer items inside your space mean fewer items to purchase, fewer things to clean and maintain, and more time to do things you really enjoy However, if you're lucky enough to find a larger place for the same price, keep in mind an extra room might facilitate live-in help or serve as a home office.

Some of us will fill our space to capacity no matter how much we have. Get rid of junk you don't need and you'll find your quarters much roomier.

STEPS TO HOME OWNERSHIP

Initially, buying a house may not be the best choice for single parents. During the early months when you're still in transition, you may feel insecure about your job or fear that you simply couldn't handle the expense of maintaining your own property. In addition, since investment returns of real estate can vary dramatically, leasing may be your best option in many locations.

Later, when you feel ready, home ownership can give you a sense of security and stability as well as provide a way to accumulate assets you can later pass on to your children.

1. **Clean up your credit act.** See Chapter 10, Deep Cleaning Your Credit Report.

2. **Prequalify.** Contact several lenders (banks, credit unions, mortgage companies) about prequalification. This step allows you to test the waters with several companies as well as give you a ballpark figure of how much you can afford to borrow.

3. **Team up with an agent and an attorney.** First-time buyers should use a licensed real estate agent to assist them in the process and an attorney at closing. A good agent will guide you through making an offer with a written contract, having the home inspected, negotiating with the owners, applying for the mortgage, and of course, the closing. Remember, the agent always represents the seller—that's who pays them

4. **Choose an agent that you trust.**

5. **Be your own advocate.** If you feel you've been discriminated against because of your status as a single parent, your gender, or your race, call your local Fair Housing Office or the national Housing and Urban Development hotline (800-669-9777).

In addition to these general steps, several agencies offer consumer information and/or referrals to outreach programs for low-to-moderate-income mortgage applicants. On the national level, contact The Fannie Mae Foundation for an excellent free booklet detailing the home ownership process (1-800-688-HOME). Fannie Mae also has a toll free line for information on mortage programs and consumer counseling (1-800-7-FANNIE). Other helpful agencies include Freddie Mac (800-373-3343) and the Mortgage Bankers Association of America (202-861-6500).

Locally, take advantage of projects by nonprofit neighborhood development corporations that buy up dilapidated housing, refurbish it, and sell it below market value in an attempt to stabilize neighborhoods. To locate such programs in your area, check with local neighborhood associations, real estate agents, or mortgage lenders.

Since the traditional 20 percent down payment and exorbitant closing costs are the major hurdles to home ownership for many, state and federal programs typically focus on ways to get people into the homes without coming up with huge chunks of money. The following measures can make your dream a reality, but make sure it's a reality you can live with.

Down payment assistance. If you qualify, your lender gives you a separate loan for the down payment amount that is underwritten by the state or federal government. You must pay this loan off in a shorter amount of time, usually about five years, in addition to your 15-year or 30-year traditional mortgage. Expense is added as you pay interest on two loans simultaneously as well as the often required mortgage insurance.

Reduction in down payment amount. Other programs simply reduce the down payment amount for qualified buyers with low incomes but good credit records. Mortgage insurance may or may not be required. You are not allowed to borrow money for the down payment, from credit cards, friends, or family. The point? Your lender does not want you to overextend yourself.

Closing costs. You can include a clause in your contract requiring the seller to pay a percentage (typically 3 percent) of the purchase price towards closing costs. If the seller agrees, it can save you from having to come up with the money on the front end to cover attorney's fees, mortgage points, and other items payable upon closing. On the downside, this maneuver will probably cut into your bargaining power to further reduce the purchase price, resulting in a higher mortgage.

Other measures are cost cutting across the board rather than just on the front end. They include:

Negotiating with the lender. Don't be afraid to shop around for lenders with the best interest rates. It is also worth your while to quibble over the 1 to 4 "points," or extra fees that are tacked on, roughly equal to .08 percent each over the life of a 30-year loan.

Choose the type of loan that fits your needs. Fixed rate mortgages are very popular when the rates are low, as they are as we go to press in the spring of 1996. Adjustable rates are more of a gamble, as they can fluctuate. Hybrids that start with a lower fixed rate, then jump to variable after a set amount of time (such as ten years) are a good bet for those who know they'll be selling before the change occurs. Beware of balloon mortgages in which your monthly payments increase dramatically during the life of the loan.

Determine if you qualify for a lower interest rate through a government program. Some government programs can lock you into a percentage rate that's slightly lower than the going rate. If you qualify, your monthly payment could be considerably lower.

Use the three-box method to sort through it all. You'll need a box for trash, a box for giveaways, and a box for items that need to be repaired. Go through each room in your house with the three boxes. If an item is broken, consider whether it's worth the trouble of fixing it before putting it in the repair box. If there is anything seriously wrong with the item, don't donate it to charity. Charities throw away thousands of pounds of donated items annually because they have no resale value. The giveaway box is for items that still have good use left in them.

After you have sorted through all your stuff, promptly throw away the trash, put the repair box in your car for the next errand day, and call Disabled American Veterans, Goodwill, Salvation Army, or your local library if you have books, to pick up the giveaway box. If you want to give friends and family a chance to go through the giveaway box, set a deadline, and if they haven't looked by that time, get rid of it. Remember, "if in doubt, throw it out."

Finally, many say that our living space is a reflection of our inner space. If you make do with a smaller home, streamline your possessions, and create easy-to-follow cleaning systems, you'll free your attention to focus on your family. Or perhaps you'll put the money you're saving toward your future goals.

Transportation

Americans have a love affair with the perceived status of their vehicles. But vehicles are expensive to purchase, maintain, and insure. According to the American Automobile Association, motorists spend an average of $6,389 annually to own and operate their cars. And they depreciate. Money poured into vehicles could do very well elsewhere.

For instance, a former consultant in my firm purchased a motorcycle instead of a car and used the money he saved to run a successful business. While a motorcycle is probably not appropriate for single parents who need to cart their kids around, it illustrates an important principle about transportation and downsizing in general. Use the least that is appropriate in your situation. For some, this means public transportation; for others, carpooling; still others will own or lease.

Leasing an automobile can be one of the best values of the nineties for certain consumers, including those who drive less than 15,000 miles annually, usually get a new car every few years, or want to drive a new car or luxury model without huge cash outlays.

> **DEALS ON WHEELS**
>
> 1. Check the blue book value when buying used cars (obtain from your insurance agent, bank, or bookstore).
> 2. Call your insurance agent for a premium quote before buying. Monthly premiums could cost more than the car note.

Toys

Toys, and an abundance of them, are a reality of modern children's lives. Between birthdays and holidays or "just because," the average family spends thousands of dollars on toys by the time a child reaches 18. Single parents must deal with trying to "fill the void of the missing parent." This feeling translates into overextending themselves on toy spending.

Experts say that basic toys are more educational. They also create less waste, use less space, and feel good. Who doesn't love standard favorites such as Raggedy Ann and Andy dolls, wooden blocks, Radio

> **FREEBIE**
>
> Write for your free copy of "Toy Safety: Guidelines for Parents" at the American Academy of Pediatrics, Dept. C-Toy Safety, Box 927, Elk Grove Village, Illinois 60009-0927. Include a self-addressed stamped business-sized envelope.

GOOD DEALS

Parents will find great deals on sports equipment at Play it Again Sports. Merchandise costs 30–50 percent below regular prices and you can trade in your used equipment when your child decides to try something new.

Parent company Grow Biz has shops for used kids clothing, musical instruments, and computers as well.

Check your local CD resale shops, where you can typically get three compact disks for the price of one new one. Again, like used paperbacks, CDs can usually be traded in.

Flyer wagons, and playground balls? Single-use glitzy toys tend to be *close-ended,* a term educators use to mean there's only one way to play with them, so they don't encourage creativity. Battery-operated toys are another problem, with replacement batteries adding to the cost and waste generated over the life of the toy.

Make the most of your kids' toys by using the three-box method to get rid of unwanted or broken toys. Then set up toy storage that enables your child to keep his or her own room tidy.

Children tire of seeing the same old toys every day and begin to ask for new things. Make the most of the toys you have by rotating them. Store some in the attic or basement or garage and bring them back periodically as "new" toys. Or rotate between your house and a relative such as grandparents. Rotation works especially well with young children, but even older kids will be delighted by the rediscovery of "old friends" they had forgotten about.

Save money on purchasing toys by buying ahead. After-Christmas clearance sales are a great time to buy birthday presents and stash them ahead for your child, or to have on hand for last minute party invitations.

CONSUMER ALERT

Think back to your first experience making a large purchase. Was it your first car in high school with your parents there for support and guidance? Or was it more recently, as you set up housekeeping as a single parent and found yourself maneuvering through a dizzying array of ads, sales fliers, and *Consumer Reports* magazines?

One of the best deals around is the *Consumer's Resource Handbook*, available free by writing the Consumer Information Center, Pueblo, CO 81009. This thick booklet is chock full of tips on everything from how to complain effectively to getting the most for your hard-earned dollars. In addition, it provides an up-to-date listing of agency watchdogs that can help you with specific problems. Armed with this information, you may avoid consumer mishaps or handle them effectively when they do arise.

Whether you've done it several times, or you're just starting out, purchasing cars, electronics, and appliances can be very intimidating. The following guidelines excerpted from Robert D. Mayer's *Power Plays: How to Negotiate, Persuade and Finesse Your Way to Success in any Situation,* should help.

> **CONSUMER AND ENVIRONMENTAL TIP:**
>
> Consider battery rechargers. The special rechargeable batteries you must buy cost about 50 percent more to begin with but will last indefinitely.

Negotiating Strategies for Large Purchases

1. It's a behavioral truth! The more time a merchant spends answering your questions (i.e., gas versus electric, measurements, models, colors, warranties, etc.), the more likely that the price or other concessions will be given to capture your business.

2. Tire and appliance stores often use so-called confidentially printed price lists to discourage bargaining. When they do, "wholesale" is seldom true cost. And as for the "manufacturer's suggested retail price," it's always a sales tool rather than a reflection of worth.

3. Nothing is sacred about a printed installment purchase agreement or sales contract. A three-part form is not immune from your negotiating a price or terms. Any agreement entitled "Standard" is designed to protect and serve only one person—the merchant who paid to have it prepared.

4. Give the merchant a face-saving exit from a fixed-price policy or a "this is our best price" offer. This technique is done by explaining why the policy shouldn't be applicable to you: "I know this is a fixed-price store, but the refrigerator on the sales floor should be priced as a 'demo'... You don't have your normal large selection of colors and models to choose from... This dryer is not in mint condition... There is a model change coming out next month."

5. "Are you competitive?" (Who will answer no?) With a yes answer, ask: "What was your lowest price when a customer discovered this model was selling for less elsewhere?" Ask: "Why shouldn't I be entitled to the same competitive price?" Ask: "Why should I be put to the task of comparative shopping?"

6. Merchants who won't or can't reduce their price will, when asked, often throw in free delivery, installation, or assembly; wave extended warranty fees; or offer extras. ("I will buy the four tires if you align and balance them at no cost.")

7. And one for the road: "What's the discount if I pay cash?"

Source: Robert D. Mayer. *Power Plays: How to Negotiate, Persuade, and Finesse Your Way to Success in Any Situation*. New York: Times Books/ Random House, 1996. By permission of the author.

This chapter should have given you plenty of ideas about how to save money by identifying your spending style, applying the principles of downsizing to your own life, and learning to stand up for your rights as a consumer. The next chapter turns to your children, the role they play in your financial life, and what you can teach them about money to contribute to their future and current prosperity.

RESOURCES

Don Aslett and Laura Aslett Simons. *Make Your House Do the Housework*. Revised ed. Cincinnati: Betterway Books, 1995.

Connie Cox and Cris Evatt. *Simply Organized: How to Simplify Your Complicated Life*. New York: Putnam, 1988.

Consumer's Resource Handbook. Write to "Handbook," Consumer Information Center, Pueblo, CO 81009.

Debra Wishik Englander. *How to Be Your Own Financial Planner.* Rocklin, CA: Prima Publishing, 1995.

Robert Mayer. *Power Plays: How to Negotiate, Persuade and Finesse Your Way to Success in Any Situation.* NewYork: Times Books/Random House, 1996.

Timothy Miller, Ph.D. *How to Want What You Have: Discovering the Magic and Grandeur of Ordinary Existence.* New York: Henry Holt, 1995.

Sue Robin. *The Smart Shopper's Guide to the Best Buys For Kids.* New York: Macmillan Spectrum, 1996.

Andrew Tobias. *The Only Investment Guide You'll Ever Need.* Revised ed. San Diego: Harcourt Brace, 1996.

CHAPTER 8

Teamwork: Getting the Kids Involved

Financially speaking, your children can be your best friends or your worst enemies. Their material wants and needs can pull against what you know is best for their future. Get them on your side and they can enthusiastically support your financial planning efforts.

All parents hate denying their children. Single parents often feel worse because they blame themselves. "Instead of remembering all the things I did give him, I felt remorseful—and guilty," said one parent. Single parents must avoid this kind of thinking, especially when it arises from a sense of one's own shortcomings.

Cultivate healthy attitudes toward money and watch your children's responsibility grow. But be forewarned. Children are not miniature adults. Don't plant seeds of insecurity by confiding all your financial woes. Strike a balance between the security they need and the honesty they deserve.

HEALTHY MONEY ATTITUDES

Money is a tool. Just as a hammer can be used to build a house or destroy one, money and the way it's used determine its effects. While money is necessary for material survival, it's not the meaning of life.

When we work for our money, we trade hours of our life for it and in turn trade the money for goods and services. Many adults never make this connection. Imagine then, how mysterious money must be to children. Money may seem like magic to them. After all, "that little card goes in the slot and out pops cash." As we rely more on abstract forms of payment such as checks, debit cards, or credit cards, the time-money-goods and services exchange concept becomes even more puzzling to them.

To form healthy attitudes toward money, it's essential that children understand the relationship between earning and spending. In the context of your family financial goals, this understanding will encourage them to make momentary material sacrifices. They'll be less likely to feel like the "poor cousin" today when they can dream of future financial rewards.

AGES AND STAGES

Remember your fourth-grade lesson on how to balance a checkbook? How about your sixth-grade lesson in budgeting? Probably not. Unfortunately, the closest we get to money management in our schools is "If Sally bought a red apple for 25 cents and a green apple for 30 cents, how much change would she get back from her dollar?" Never mind where the dollar was earned, what sales tax would be charged, or whether Sally had the option of saving her dollar in a piggy bank. With few exceptions, school money talk is relegated to abstract math problems or hinted at in social studies discussions of capitalism.

In addition, studies show that children understand their world differently at different ages. Whether you are teaching your children the fundamentals of money management or sharing details about your family finances, you should be sensitive to their changing needs. In general treat money questions like sex questions. Answer directly, honestly, and specifically what's being asked. There's no need to elaborate. If the child wants to know more, the child will ask.

The following list of developmental stages provides guidelines for what children are ready to hear about your own family finances and what they're ready to learn about money management.

American children aged 6–17 receive over $45 billion a year in disposable income from allowances, gifts, and jobs. They spend most of it on food, entertainment, and clothes.
—Source: The Nickelodeon Yankelovich Youth Monitor, ™ 1995

Infant and Toddler

Child psychologists agree that children under age three can be affected by disruptions in their familiar routines. You may find that your financial woes are reflected in their behavior, such as regressions to earlier comfort habits such as thumb sucking. Reassure them with comforting statements such as, "We are going through a difficult time, but we are safe and I love you." Although very young children may not understand the meanings of the words you say, they'll find comfort in your facial expressions and tone of voice.

This readiness period is a good time to lay the foundation of financial understanding by describing your money transactions in simple words: "I am giving the man behind the counter five dollars to pay for this Sesame Street toy" or "We are letting the bank hold our money for us, so it will be safe until we need it." Help children begin to associate the names of coins and bills with their relative value: "A quarter is worth 25 cents. I can use it to buy a banana or a pencil."

Preschool

Already missing one parent, three- to six-year-olds can be acutely sensitive to abandonment issues and need extra reassurance. Reassure your preschoolers that you'll always try to be there for them but if you're not there they will be taken care of. Keep the focus on where they would go and who would take care of them in your absence.

Other financial concerns should be openly discussed when they directly affect the child. For instance, if you must work longer hours to support the family, tell your children, so they'll understand about the extra hours they're spending in day care or after-school programs. If you have to downsize by moving to a less expensive residence, the children have a right to know why they're moving or changing schools. In a true crisis such as a job loss, it's important to be honest without scaring the children. Remember, even when the truth is awful, the children were probably imagining something far worse.

Three- to six-year-olds can also grasp the value of money. A small weekly allowance (especially if "earned" by doing light chores) can reinforce the relationship between earning and spending, as well as introduce budgeting. Make it a practice to tell your child how much money you've decided to spend before going into a store. As you're shopping, you can add up items aloud, ensuring that you stay within your budget. Be sure to show your child if you choose less expensive alternatives and explain why. At this age, budgeting can seem like a fun game. It's your chance to teach a valuable lesson.

School-age

Because 6- to 12-year-olds are no longer babies, we tend to endow them with maturity that shouldn't be reasonably expected. Avoid the temptation to confide your financial woes to your children. They are still egocentric enough to think that somehow they're responsible for the situation. They are apt to worry extensively about it and may "clam up" about their own problems because they don't want to worry you further. But don't follow in the footsteps of the previous generation, where finances weren't considered appropriate for general discussion. Your children will learn from your example. If they see you acknowledge your financial problems and rise to work through them, they'll learn to do the same.

In school, your child is learning about money denominations and how to make change. When shopping together, reinforce school lessons by asking your school-age children to estimate how much change they'll get back from the cashier and by helping them count the returned change.

By school-age, a regular allowance is a wise investment in your child's financial future. Although school-age children are ready for more financial responsibility, they may still be challenged by the idea of delayed gratification.

Start small by having them choose a toy to save for that's worth two weeks' allowance. The first week, remind them that they wanted to save for the toy. Refer often to a picture of the toy to prevent waning enthusiasm. (Remember, two weeks is a long time even for an eight-year-old.) Avoid the temptation to advance the money because your objective is to encourage waiting. The second week, plan to go with your child on a special trip to triumphantly claim the hard-earned prize. Praise the effort. Perhaps she'll want to save for an even bigger item next time.

WALDO'S BEST MONEY TIPS FOR OTHER KIDS

1. You know you're at an expensive restaurant when the waiters are men.

2. Order what you want from room service and don't try to make it fit the menu. (Ask if they have kid meals.)

3. When your mom or dad is renting a car, ask the rental person for a free upgrade to a van or station wagon, which usually costs twice as much. (If they have plenty in stock and a kid asks, they might give it to you.)

4. Buy your snacks from vending machines because it's easier and faster and your mom or dad doesn't have to plan ahead. The only problem is it costs more that way and your snack might get stuck coming out.

5. T-shirts. I don't buy souvenir T-shirts everywhere I go because they cost too much and I don't need them.

6. My mom buys me three to five pairs of shoes ahead (in 1/2 size increments) at the Nike factory outlet because they cost less there; then I don't have to go back and shop again, plus I like to see what size I'm going to be growing into next. I like to organize them and put them away.

7. If you go to a hotel, ask for a corporate discount, a business room, and a free upgrade.

8. Ordering pizza: Get coupons from the newspaper. If you don't have a coupon, ask what their daily special is.

9. My mom and I used to rent four or five videos at a time because we couldn't agree. But we found out we were wasting money because we didn't watch them all. Now we get two movies—one that I like and one for both of us.

10. I don't get money out of my mom's purse without asking her. You get more if you just ask.

11. Savings: I take some money from my piggy bank and my mom makes it into a check and mails it to the bank for me with my name and my savings book. They send my savings book back. Save your allowance and make your mom or dad pay for everything. I'm saving mine for college, and if there's enough left over I'll get a car and a mansion.

12. Chores: I earn money by doing chores like taking out the trash, putting water in the garden fountain, and emptying or filling the dishwasher. It's good for little kids to do something to earn an allowance.

Open a savings account for your school-age child if you haven't done so already. Introduce the concept of interest and be sure to go over each statement as well as to make special trips to the bank for depositing. If your bank still uses passbooks, let the child be responsible for keeping track of it.

Teenage

As a part of growing into adulthood, teenagers naturally begin to disengage from the family identity, seeking greater and greater independence. Teenage children of single parents may hesitate with this step and try to align strongly with the family either out of insecurity or out of a need to compensate for the missing parent. This response is normal in the context of a transition while the family is pulling together, but watch it closely and don't let it hinder development. In the alternative, teenagers may slip into the background, unnoticed. While your attention is turned to other more "pressing" demands, your teenager might be on the road to trouble, which can be costly to your wallet and your heart.

Whether you are encouraging your teen's independence or discouraging withdrawal, it's appropriate to start a constructive involvement in the family finances.

Show teenagers where to find important papers such as your will, insurance policies, and power of attorney. They are mature enough to share in your financial planning, especially concerning their own futures. However, keep resisting that temptation to dump adult information in their laps. They are growing up so fast already, give them time to savor their last glimpses of childhood.

If you permit your teen to work for extra money, be sure to lay firm ground rules to ensure that work won't interfere with school. *The greatest investment you can make in your child's future (financially and otherwise) is to facilitate a successful school experience.* Although you might be tempted to rationalize that the teen's job is supplementing your family income, you must realize that you're making a serious trade-off with the child's future. Try other survival strategies before you allow work to interfere with school.

Under the right circumstances work experience can be valuable if you use it to teach basic money management skills. Require a certain percentage to be saved for "larger goodies" and a certain percentage to be put in a special college savings account. (More on this in Chapter 12, "Planning for College.")

Older teens with money from allowances and jobs will be ready for a checking account. Make it a joint account if you feel the need to keep an eye on their transactions. Avoid the temptation to bail them out if they overspend. A trademark of adolescence is learning things the hard way. Let them be accountable for their actions now, so they'll be responsible for their actions later.

Young Adult

During the college years you should be ready to open adult lines of communication about your finances. Whether you have planned for college expenses or are frantically scrambling for your options, your offspring is ready to take on a greater role. During this transition the financial baton is passed on to your offspring. Be clear about your mutual expectations. Do you expect the student to work during these years to supplement what you've saved? Will you take out student loans? Who is expected to pay back the loans? How many years will you foot the bill?

If the young adult is not entering higher education, you must decide how long you're willing to support him or her. If he or she is living at home, you should draw up an informal agreement about living arrangements. Will rent be paid? Who will purchase food and sundries? Will he or she contribute to home and yard maintenance? How will he or she entertain friends? Who will provide a means of transportation, insurance, and so forth? If your child is away from home, be clear from the start whether moving back home is an option or whether you're willing to supplement the child's income.

With cash machines on every corner and a new sense of freedom, the temptations of campus life can strain your child's financial fitness. Many banks offer products targeted for students, from student checking that allows the parent to make deposits from another city, to student credit cards that are jointly held by the parents and students but allow

COLLEGE CHECKLIST

Cash: Open a student checking account and determine guidelines.

Credit: Apply for student credit card. Determine who will pay the bill, what items are acceptable for charging, and so forth.

Insurance: Theft is the number-one crime on college campuses. Your homeowner's policy probably covers belongings in a dorm room if your home is listed as your child's permanent address on his or her driver's license and voter registration. Off-campus or student housing requires purchasing a "renter's insurance" agreement. Either way, just as when at home, you should "schedule" large-ticket items such as computer or music systems (pay an extra fee with your premium to waive the deductible on those high-risk items). Check other policies such as auto and health to see if they will change under the new circumstances.

Telephone: Choose a long-distance calling option. Consider a calling card, or if long distance calls are to be limited to calling home, get a personal 1-800 number that will allow your child to call home toll free from any phone.

students to earn credit in their name. Help your child obtain these tools and use them wisely.

If your young adult has led a sheltered financial life, you will need to walk your child through the basics of writing a check and balancing the account with a monthly statement. One college freshman admitted that he was confused when the balance shown on his cash machine statement was often larger than the balance in his checkbook register. It took a bounced check and a sympathetic banker to help him realize that the inflated balances were a result of "floating" checks that hadn't been posted to his account; not some electronic windfall.

THE FAMILY AS A TEAM

As a single parent, you're acting as the owner, coach, and cheerleader of your family team. Teaching your children to be team players will add to the harmony of your family and to their success in society. Being a team player yourself means that you'll put the needs of your children first when it comes to dealing with their other parent even if those dealings are uncomfortable for you.

The Parent's Role as Coach

You are the glue that holds your family team together. You need a game plan to run your team successfully. We hope that by this point in the book you have a good idea of who you are, where you're going, and how you plan to get there. Now you need to share that with the children in their own language. While you will want to avoid "taking away their childhood" by imposing too much responsibility, you must face the reality that things won't run smoothly without their cooperation.

Confront your children's tendency to assume the blame for family troubles. They must understand that they aren't to blame for the missing parent's absence. In an angry moment, five-year-old Jeremy wished his mother was dead. Later, when she was killed in a tragic accident, he actually thought he had caused her death. Psychologists call this "magic thinking," and it affects children whose parents leave for divorce or separation as well. Through actions and words, you must assure your children that the missing parent and financial difficulties are not their fault. Don't involve your child in arguments about money with your spouse. Never complain about a "deadbeat" spouse to your child. However, you can empower children by showing them the difference between taking the blame for actions that are beyond their control and being responsible for situations they *can* change.

Sports teams use "defensive" strategies to maintain the ground they've accomplished and prevent further negative changes in their position. "Offensive" strategies are used for gaining ground or scoring points. The winning team is the one that knows how and when to use the appropriate strategy. Both are necessary to win.

In family dynamics, one can think of two different kinds of skills. "Defensive" skills are those essential to basic survival and the "offensive" skills make survival worthwhile. Cultural expectations largely determine what goes into each category, but most Americans would agree on the following divisions:

Defensive/survival: regular nutritious meals; clean, dry, safe, and disease-free living quarters; *necessary* medical and dental care; transportation; an income sufficient to obtain these things.

Offensive/enrichment: a complete education (12th grade or higher) for yourself and your children; *preventative* medical and dental care; caring relationships with family and friends; pleasant living quarters; time to play; family traditions and rituals; a spiritual practice (although many will argue that this belongs on the other list); a secure retirement; income from a job or career that brings joy to your life.

Many single parents get stuck on the defensive. They survive day by day, and feel "But for what?" This list could as well be called "chores to be completed to keep the family running smoothly." And unfortunately, the list is general and far from inclusive. Each item can be broken into several manageable chunks. "Regular nutritious meals" becomes "grocery shop, chop vegetables, make soup, pack lunch boxes, wash dishes, and so forth" or occasionally, "order pizza," depending on the mood you're in. "Clean, dry, safe, and disease-free living quarters" could mean "hire a plumber, make sure the kids don't hide pizza under their beds, nag the landlord about the leaky roof, clean the bathroom, mop the floor, remove the cobwebs from my lingerie drawer." The lists go on just as the number of people to complete them has dwindled.

If you're stuck on the defensive, find ways to do your "defensive" duties more efficiently, so you can move to the offensive. For example, buy prechopped vegetagles in the supermarket. Cook and freeze emergency meals or find a healthy take-out nearby. Gain ground by streamlining your systems (see "Downsizing" in Chapter 7) and delegating appropriately to other team members (i.e., your kids). Be committed to gaining ground for the sake of your own and your children's futures.

Even if your family consists of only two people, like mine, it helps to keep the lines of communication open through regular family meetings. Meetings serve a dual purpose of empowering your child and monitoring the changing aspects of your "family economy." Kids love giving advice, and you'll be surprised at what their fresh perspectives will uncover.

Children have a natural tendency to get enthusiastic about issues that affect them and the ability to make changes in their own lives. Make your family their new "cause." You'll be delighted at what you can accomplish together.

The Kids as Team Players

Just as it's in your children's best interest if you get along with their other parent, it's in your family's best interest if the children get along with one another. Now that they are vying for only one parent's attention, sibling rivalry can become intensified. In some cases, children take sides with one parent or the other. If children are on different sides, everyone loses. What does this have to do with finances? Believe me, any disruptions in family harmony will make their way straight to your wallet.

Combat sibling rivalry with big doses of love and attention from you. Be sure to leave a little time each day to interact with each child individually.

RESOURCES

Janet Bodnar. *Mom, Can I Have That? Dr. Tightwad Answers Your Kid's Questions About Money.* New York: Random House, 1996.

Neale S. Godfrey and Carolina Edwards. *Money Doesn't Grow on Trees.* New York: Simon & Schuster, 1995.

Neale S. Godfrey and Tad Richards. *A Penny Saved: Using Money to Teach Your Children the Way the World Works.* New York: Simon & Schuster, 1995.

Neale S. Godfrey and Tad Richards. *From Cradle to College (and Everything In Between): Planning the Financial Future You'll Share with Your Children.* New York: HarperCollins, 1996.

Vicki Lansky. *The Divorce Book for Parents.* New York: Signet, 1989.

CHAPTER 9

The Missing Parent

Ideally, parents are responsible for their children's *financial* and *emotional* well-being. Sometimes, one parent chooses to drop the ball in one or both of these categories, leaving the other parent and the kids high and dry. Call them deadbeats. Call them worse. However angry their behavior makes you, for the children, the psychological costs of a missing parent can't be measured in money.

You, who are acting as a responsible adult, may find yourself having to hold your tongue for the sake of your children. Unless your former spouse is physically dangerous to you and to them, children need both parents. Your challenge: Battle for what your children deserve while keeping your own cool.

This chapter gives a step-by-step process to getting child support while balancing the value of the money with the value of keeping the missing parent involved. Stories of parents who are at different stages in the process provide creative and successful solutions. We'll also take a look at their mistakes to help you avoid the same traps.

Later, we'll look at more statistics, but remember, statistics are only head counts of a population. With awareness and choice, there's no need for you to despair even if the other parent is a POW (prisoner of war) of a new marriage or is MIA (missing in action) and stays missing. Many helpful resources exist to help you and your child fill in the parenting blank.

> **The percentage of children living with only one parent more than doubled between 1970 and 1993, from 8.2 million to 17.6 million.**
> —Source: 1993 Census

CULTIVATING CONSTRUCTIVE RELATIONSHIPS

The emotional and financial payoffs of getting along with the other parent of your child can't be overemphasized. Keep relationships cordial

When the elephants
fight, it's the grass
that suffers.
—WEST AFRICAN
PROVERB

even when the divorce wasn't easy. Your children will suffer if you and your ex turn them into a battleground.

Santa Monica, California, family law attorney Susan Weiss wisely said, "You can't force your ex-husband to be a good parent." If your former spouse is bent on disappearing, there's probably no way you can stop him or her. Some people aren't cut out for the difficult, continuous work of nurturing a child. No amount of coaxing or playing on feelings of guilt will help.

A professional man tells this story—his wife lost interest in the children and refused to call or visit with them. Despite his efforts to set up visitation, nothing worked. Six-year-old Andy still had bed-wetting problems. When Andy went to a friend's sleep-over birthday party, they had to hide the fact that Andy still wore diapers. It doesn't take a trained psychotherapist to see the link between the bed-wetting and the missing mother.

Other parents face different problems. Joint custody brings its own set of budgetary woes. If your life involves a patchwork of week-on and week-off parenting, it's particularly hard to arrange for continuity in childcare. You may find yourself squashing work into one week, child errands into the next. No matter what the arrangements, study after study shows that children need two parents. When a parent is missing, the psychological and financial costs to the child and society mount. Your defense? Provide strong adult role models as surrogates through close friends, relatives, or organizations such as Big Brothers and Big Sisters.

Parenting Styles

Agreeing on parenting styles provokes many people into battles over deep-held values that pass from generation to generation in a family. An added twist, many people reject their own parents' styles and try to achieve the opposite with mixed results.

As I was planning an out-of-town writing meeting with my co-author, the issue of whether to take our children arose. I had to take my son Waldo because he was due at a gymnastics competition in a nearby city. Christie wanted to take her daughter Arabella since she was still nursing and had never spent the night with her baby-sitter. Emily had trouble understanding why Arabella couldn't stay home, while Christie couldn't figure out how Emily could have been leaving Waldo behind since he was younger. Both of us got pretty fired up in the heated exchange of faxes (it was a writing day so we weren't supposed to be on the telephone).

Now consider how much harder this kind of exchange becomes when you've separated or divorced. Probably one of the issues you fought over concerned parenting decisions. When these issues— whether to leave the child for a business trip, how much allowance to pay, or when to begin toilet training—arise between the two of you, you often find yourself refighting old battles. Contending with the change of styles can be difficult for the child and devastating for you.

The changes of styles can be compounded by shifting attitudes expressed toward one parent by another. Children need to love the parent they are living with free from anxiety and knowing that loving one parent doesn't mean denouncing the other. Yet parents often ask just this as they make cutting remarks about the other spouse. From payment of child support to Christmas crises, leave the adult stuff to the adults. Just as Christie and Emily would resolve their travel plans without drawing Arabella and Waldo into the fray, you and your former spouse must settle issues about which you disagree outside the presence of the child.

Controlling emotions in such situations proves taxing, but the adults concerned must try, for the children's sake, to keep their negative feelings to themselves. If not, remaining family ties are undermined and children suffer the loss of important emotional supports in their lives.

RESOURCES FOR SINGLE PARENTS

Big Brothers and Big Sisters of America
230 North 13th Street
Philadelphia, PA 19107
215-567-7000

National Center for Missing and Exploited Children
1835 K. Street, NW,
Suite 700
Washington, DC 20006
202-634-9821 or
800-843-5678

Handbook on parental abductions.

Parents Without Partners
401 North Michigan Avenue
Chicago, IL 60611-4267
800-637-7974

The Single Parents Association
4727 Bell Road,
Suite 45-209
Phoenix, AZ 85032
602-788-5511
800-704-2102
(outside of Arizona)
E-mail:
SPA@NETA.COM

SUSTAINING CHILD SUPPORT PAYMENTS

Statistics aren't on your side here either. Only one-third of divorces resulted in child support being awarded to the custodial parent, that is, the parent with custody of the children. As low as this number sounds, the facts worsen as time passes. After a year, only about three-fourths of the awards are still being paid; after five years, the figure dips to only two-thirds.

The news isn't good if one-third of all solo mothers had to use the federal government to help with gaining child support. *One of the tenets of this book is that you should try, if at all possible, to provide in whole or in part for you and your children.* If the experience doesn't convince you, these statistics might. If you are able to obtain alimony and child support, reserve it for college, savings, investments, and retirement. That way you'll be able to stay even if the bottom drops out of the child and spousal support floor.

In Chapter 2, we looked at the dissolution and settlement process. Assuming that you read this book before the completion of the process, we hope that, with your attorney's help, you followed our suggestions and were able to obtain a reasonable financial settlement.

If not, or if your settlement came but child and spousal support have been interrupted or if they're too low, here's how to return to enforce your support or negotiate for more.

MONTHLY BILLING TRICK

Type up and photocopy a year's supply and write the current date as you send the child support "bill" each month.

Informal Collections

If your spouse doesn't send payments regularly on schedule, try sending a monthly bill, so your invoice sits in the same pile as the other creditors'. To make it so easy it's embarrassing, include a stamped, self-addressed return envelope.

To safeguard the validity of your future court case, it is also extremely important to keep a running list of the payments you do receive. Photocopy checks and list the date, check number, and amount of each payment. Cash payments should be recorded as well. In his firm's booklet, *The Client's Guide to Divorce*, family practice lawyer R. Miles Mason asserts, "If you cannot prove what you *did* get, the court might not believe you when you testify about what you *did not* get [emphasis added]."

As a preventative measure, avoid making verbal agreements with your ex and never sign any documents that your lawyer hasn't approved. No matter how well you get along, your verbal agreements about changes in alimony or child support payments can get you in trouble.

If informal tactics such as these don't work, don't put your children in the role of collectors. While it's very difficult to restrain oneself when an idolized other parent continues not to do his/her financial part, the only damage you'll do will be to your kids' image of you—and of themselves. They'll think of you as a nag and themselves as unworthy of receiving support.

GET IT IN WRITING

When Mary Sandberg's ex got a big promotion and raise, they were getting along famously. Rather than going to the trouble to file for a court-ordered change in child support, they reached an informal agreement that he would pay an extra $1,000 per month. He kept it up for a few months, then started slipping. She decided to sue him for the "back money he owed her" and found that although the judge sympathized, under the law all she could do was order the higher amount to be paid from this point on.

Instead, turn to your family law attorney. Get your attorney to try to enforce the agreement through writing a letter to jog your ex into paying. If that approach fails, don't wait long before filing contempt charges against your ex. The longer you wait, the harder it will be to collect delinquent support. If your ex is more than a month behind in payments yet still employed, your charges may lead to wage assignment and ultimately jail time in extreme cases. In wage assignment, the employer must pay the child support directly to the county clerk (it will show as a deduction on your ex's pay stub), who will then pay it to you. Such improved state controls have resulted from national media attention on "deadbeat dads" as well as an ongoing battle women and their attorneys have fought for years.

NEGOTIATING MORE SUPPORT

A small change in salary can trigger changes in child support, but it's up to you to file a court order for the increased amount. Don't rely on the generosity of the obligor. Even if larger payments are made for awhile, they can always fall back on the minimum requirements in your original decree. If you don't have it in writing, the spouse doesn't owe you an extra cent. It's better to get the court order for the larger amount as soon as possible. Monitor income by obtaining a copy of the yearly tax return.

State Courts

To increase spousal support and alimony, you'll have to return to the court where you received your dissolution or to a new court if you have changed residencies. A word of caution here: Marital law is very much state-law based. Under the constitution, each state can and does make its own laws that reflect, among other things, historical antecedents and current social and economic outlooks. To complicate matters further, local courts have their own rules and procedural requirements. Some states, such as New York and California, have enlightened views about dissolution or divorce and accompanying those views, strong support and enforcement mechanisms.

In California, a community property state, traditionally, settlements exceed those of most states, but when it comes to spousal support, the numbers show a decline since the 1970s. Child support has followed suit, but the curve is less steep. For a woman divorcing after a *long-term* California marriage, defined as exceeding 10 years, the chances of getting spousal support aren't as great as the chances of getting child support. Once spousal support is awarded, *the courts must retain formal jurisdiction over it* to obtain a new review. Be careful if you seek dissolution in California that the courts have retained jurisdiction. This jurisdiction doesn't have to be retained to obtain increased child support; the courts assume you may need to return.

As with the initial divorce process, you and your former spouse will have to provide a detailed budget picture, including your income from earnings; other income such as interest; your assets such as house, furniture, and art; monthly living expenses, including rent, utilities, food, transportation, childcare, health costs; and debt.

The judge uses a sophisticated computer program to determine how much support each parent should be paying. If your spouse's contribution should be higher, according to the formula, then you're likely to obtain more support. However, if your former spouse has taken on new obligations, such as a new family, or is earning less, whether from a change of jobs, starting a business, or even an illness, this information becomes a variable in the equation.

Depending on the changes that have occurred on the other side, you could find yourself with a smaller award. To avoid this possibility, if at all feasible, your attorney will want to "run the numbers" first. Of course, if your spouse is sufficiently uncooperative as to warrant a return to court, he or she may be hard to pin down outside a courtroom about financial changes. While you'll certainly know if more children are in the family photo album, it's unlikely you'll know the size of your ex's paycheck or debts especially if several years have passed.

> ## STATE HELP
>
> Check the government blue pages in your local phone book under the State Department of Human Services for the Office of Child-Support Enforcement (name may vary).

Other states more wedded to past realities than to current trends fail to provide for as much in the way of support, collection, and enforcement.

One Mother's Confession: "I wasn't good at getting child support and asked for no alimony, and because I've been self-sustaining since I turned 21, I expect that experience colored my willingness and ability to forego more child support in favor of keeping the lines of communication open.

"After negotiations stalled completely when I asked for normal child support from my husband, my attorney and I settled on $50 a month, so that my child would have some sense of his father's contributing to his well-being. I have yet to make my monthly goal of actually showing my son the check, so that he won't feel economically abandoned by his father. The reason: The first check has yet to arrive."

Will this mother take her ex-husband through the federal collection process? Probably not. The loss of cooperation would far outweigh the monetary value.

RESOURCES

Child Support Legal Resource Kit, NOW Legal Defense and Education Fund (available from NOW Legal Defense and Education Fund, 99 Hudson Street, New York NY 10013).

Constance R. Ahrons and Roy H. Rogers. *Divorce Families: Meeting the Challenge of Divorce and Remarriage*. New York: W. W. Norton, 1989.

Linda Foust. *The Single Parent's Almanac*. Rocklin, CA: Prima Publishing, 1996.

Stephen P. Herman. *Parent vs. Parent: How You and Your Child Can Survive the Custody Battle*. New York: Pantheon, 1990.

Carl J. Hoffman. *Dead Beat Dads: How to Find Them and Make Them Pay*. New York: Simon & Schuster, 1996.

Robin Leonard and Stephen Elias. *Nolo's Pocket Guide to Family Law, Third Edition*. Berkeley: Nolo Press, 1994.

Gordon B. Plumb and Mary E. Lindley. *Humanizing Child Custody Disputes: The Family's Team*. Springfield, Ill: Charles C. Thomas, 1990.

Judith S. Wallerstein and Sandra Blakeslee. *Second Chances: Men, Women, and Children, a Decade After Divorce*. Boston: Houghton Mifflin, 1990.

CHAPTER 10

Coping with Financial Emergencies

Short of severe ill health, nothing can be more debilitating than an acute financial emergency, especially one that turns into a chronic financial crisis. When we're already on edge, almost anything can set off a feeling of financial crisis. From overtipping by five dollars and realizing it in bed that night to finding ourselves hounded by collectors, our responses will be dictated by a combination of the external realities and our internal landscape.

In truth, overtipping or paying too much for an item later on sale, while aggravating, cannot truly be classified as a financial crisis. Our response might include overamping and entering crisis mode, but actually our response isn't in this case related to reality. Before you go ballistic, do an internal check and be sure that the crisis of the moment really is a crisis.

For example, on the way out the door to work, you may pull your bills out of the mailbox and see that if your utilities aren't paid by the 24th, your lights will be shut off. It's the 15th, you have money in the bank, and you need to pay the bill. Is this a crisis worthy of turning around and racing into the house to write out a check? No. Do it tonight. Don't throw off your day by a minor annoyance.

On the other hand, if you open the mailbox and see that your mortgage goes into foreclosure tomorrow and you're fresh out of funds, you rightly might categorize the situation as a crisis. But wait. Foreclosures require months of work on a lender's part to throw you out on the street.

Is this good for your credit? No. Can you ignore this notice? No. Will you come home tonight to find your personal belongings lining the curb? No. Toughen up. To survive as a single parent, sometimes we have to play the system. Even without money, often payables can be stretched over weeks, months, or even years, buying us time to recoup.

The newly separated or divorced find themselves particularly vulnerable to overextension. Single father Bernard Bates said it best, "If you're a single parent, you've probably maxed out a credit card or two." While expenses have soared and income has dropped, so too feelings of inadequacy rise while self-esteem drops. Shopping won't cure any of these problems, but sometimes in moments of anguish we forget ourselves and turn to bingeing, whether in clothing shops or record shops as a way to stave off the feeling of helplessness. Unfortunately, out-of-control spending only leads to more problems and more depression.

Other spending seems unavoidable but can drive one into financial quicksand. Unexpected medical needs; expenses necessary to provide family support and counseling; or new housing, automobile, or furniture needs to replace those lost in a divorce settlement are just a few examples.

Divorce is an especially risky time for potential bankruptcies. Ruptures in the fabric of the family, tugs of war carried out in the bank account as the marriage falters, and the sheer cost of setting up two families lead many divorcing couples into bankruptcy. Before you take that step, study the pointers here. But if bankruptcy becomes the only way out, don't beat yourself over the head.

CREDIT CRISIS

Worrying about unpaid bills and fending off creditors present some of the worst experiences known in our consumer-driven society. While it's best to avoid being caught short, there are times when a credit crunch becomes inevitable. Credit shortages happen to our national economy, so it's not surprising that individual budgets experience them too.

In the past when institutions faced tight money, they rarely lost their credit but had to pay more for it. Nowadays, as we've seen in the Orange County, California, bankruptcy, counties and even the federal government can see funds dry up overnight. But after a governmental credit crisis, the penalty isn't nearly so severe as that for individuals. Once you get one or two black marks on your credit report, you quickly lose the ability to take on new credit at any price.

Ironically, when national credit cycles reduce credit, individuals and businesses suffer smaller, trickle-down crunches. Car loans become harder to negotiate, and the small business loan market dries up. Sometimes, economic downturns exacerbate your own personal turn of fortunes.

Whatever the reason, your response to a credit problem should start with a damage assessment. How would you characterize your problem?

- A temporary, short-term inability to meet your current obligations.

- A loss of income set off by your divorce, unemployment, business failure, or investment losses, resulting in a need for a six-month to one-year plan to recover.

- A possible need for bankruptcy code protection, when your debt so far outstrips your ability to pay that you need legal help.

- A case of fraud, a serious situation in which your past exaggerations or even your spouse's financial sins—while you were married—catch up with you.

Your response to the crisis should be tailored to its severity.

Short-Term Credit Crunch

A short-term crunch means you reasonably expect that you'll be able to bring your debts current in 60 to 90 days. Your goal here: To keep your credit and credit rating secure while you recover.

Short-term tactics:

- ☑ List all bills.

- ☑ Note due dates and grace periods.

- ☑ Pay bills only at the end of the grace period—the computer doesn't know the difference, as long as the payment reaches the creditor before the "late" period.

- ☑ Send only the minimum due, but pay something on all your bills. Don't pay all of some bill and none on another.

- ☑ Don't charge anything on cards that are due in 30 days, such as American Express or Diners Club.

Your immediate posture centers on convincing your creditors that you're operating as usual. If you use these credit-stretching tactics to preserve your credit rating, a short-term credit crunch won't leave you with damaged credit for years to come.

Medium-Term Credit Crisis

A crisis that could extend beyond your ability to stretch your credit calls for a different response. Rather than spreading your remaining resources around, you need to prioritize in a process similar to emergency room triage. For the sake of the most salvageable "patients," you'll need to let some of your credit "die."

The first cut should depend on creditors' responses; the more cooperative the creditor, the greater your benefit from paying something, however small.

Call or write creditors with an explanation that you've met difficulties, you intend to pay your bills, and ask for their cooperation.

INSULATING YOURSELF FROM THOSE PESKY COLLECTORS

Assert your legal rights with collectors. Collectors have no right to call you early in the morning or late at night. They have no right to call you at work once you have asked them not to in writintg. For that matter, once you ask not to be called *in writing* creditors cannot call you unless they intend to take more formal legal steps.

Creditors and collectors all too often violate these procedures, so log any calls you receive, noting the time and date, and use this evidence against the collector. Many a consumer debt has been forgiven in exchange for consumers' not suing overly agressive collectors.

Also, get an answering machine and use it to filter unwanted calls. You have no obligation to talk to hordes of angry collectors, thereby making your mental outlook more difficult.

Call people you know personally, such as doctors, local stores, and others where you need continuing services, and try to work out payment plans that keep the relationship alive.

Get your credit report and monitor who's on your case. If accounts are missing from the report, the likelihood is strong that the creditor won't report you for a while.

Making the choice about what to keep current and what to let slide can be excruciating because once you've defaulted on bills, creditors will call. If you aren't able to pay within a period, their efforts escalate, depending on other factors. If you have a home that can be attached or a salary that can be garnished, creditors will persist and may even take you to court. On the other hand, if your resources are scant, stonewalling may produce an end to active efforts.

The creditor may use credit-reporting services and property reports obtained from county recording offices to find your assets. However, in most instances, consumers, not computers, tell creditors exactly what they need to know.

To receive a free copy of the informative brochure "Managing Your Debts: How to Regain Financial Health," send a self-addressed stamped business-sized envelope to Consumer Federation of America, P.O. Box 12099, Washington, DC 20005-0999. Or access the brochure online at Visa's World Wide Web site: http://www/visa.com.

Deep Cleaning Your Credit Report

First, a quick primer: There are three major agencies that probably have a report in your name on file. They may even have more than one report, if you've used different versions of your name in the past or moved a lot. Their business is to keep track of the facts in your life that would help potential creditors make a decision about whether you're a good credit risk. Where do they get such personal information about you? From major creditors who inform them of open credit lines and the balances you owe, if you pay late or not at all, and finally, if they are forced to collect the debt from you.

Here's a case where what you don't know *can* hurt you. There are two ways the information contained in your credit report can be harmful.

> **Scenario #1: Their fault.** With millions of reports in existence, clerical and computer mix-ups can have dreadful consequences. The most common victims are folks with similar names or social security numbers who get damaging

entries meant for someone else's report. Other mistakes are seemingly random—flukes that can cost you dearly. If you've never seen your report, you may have been turned down for such incorrect information without even knowing it.

Scenario #2: Your fault. I'm talking about those of you who do have some skeletons in your credit closet. Entries indicating late payments, loan defaults, debt collections, or bankruptcy can send potential creditors running. But there are actions that you can take now to minimize the damage, including requesting that harmful entries be removed after seven years from the time they were first posted (ten for bankruptcy) and filing a 100-word-or-less statement telling your side of the story while the harmful records remain (credit bureaus are required to send these statements to future inquirers).

Federal law allows you to order a free copy of your credit report after it's been used to deny you credit, but then it's often too late to be of help. Instead, order your reports now for a nominal fee (around $8) from Equifax Credit Information (800-685-1111 or 770-612-2500) and Trans Union Corp. (316-636-6100 or 770-396-0961). The third major firm, TRW Credit Data, will supply you with one free copy each year regardless of whether you've been turned down for credit (800-682-7654 or 800-392-1122). It's a good idea to take care of this well in advance of applying for major credit such as a car loan or mortgage, and then to periodically reinspect your reports as a preventative measure. I suggest doing it with your annual financial check-up when you review your budget and do your taxes.

What to do with your reports when you get them:

1. Verify that your name, current home address, employer, and (if applicable) salary are up-to-date.

2. Insure that individual accounts of your ex-spouse are not listed. (If you had joint accounts when you were married, they may stay on your report for some time.)

3. Check for incomplete information such as paid-off or closed accounts that are still listed as open or unpaid.

PAYING OFF YOUR CREDIT CARD DEBT

1. It's impossible to pay off your debt if you're still adding to it. Danger sign: you're making only minimum payments on credit cards yet adding to the balances on a daily basis. If your expenses are at a bare minimum and you still can't make it, you may need to turn to community agencies, churches, or even the government for help (see Appendix 1: Accessing Government Financial Assistance).

2. Once you stop adding to your balances, you should begin paying them down. Chances are you haven't been lowering the balances at all—often the minimum payment covers little more than interest. Choose one of two strategies:

   Strategy #1: Determine the highest-rate card and set a goal to pay it off in a specific amount of time. If you owe $1,200 and you want to pay it off in a year, you should pay $100 per month. Meanwhile, continue paying the minimum on the remaining cards without adding to the balances.

   Strategy #2: If the balance on your highest-rate card seems unobtainable, give yourself a psychological lift by paying off the card with the smallest balance first. If you owe $253 on your Sears Charge, for example, you may be able to pay it off in a couple of months as opposed to the year-long commitment required by the example above. Not only will it feel good to write the final check to pay off your account, but you will have reduced the number of monthly payments you have to make, resulting in one fewer check to write and a little extra money to funnel towards another account.

3. As you pay off your cards keep only the accounts with the lowest rates and best features, such as no annual fee or free car rental insurance.

4. If your credit is good enough that you continue to receive preapproved offers for low-interest credit cards, transfer balances from higher cards but be sure to close the high-interest accounts.

A single father used this method to eliminate seven of his thirteen credit cards. He still owes a substantial debt, but it is now concentrated in several low-interest credit cards. On the months when he finds he can afford only the minimum payments, his debt service (which used to run around $500 monthly) is a much more manageable $200.

4. Check for accounts or other information that you don't recognize. Most commonly due to mistakes, they could also result from fraudulent accounts set up illegally by third parties using your credit information.

5. Examine negative entries that are true. Even if you can't dispute them, make sure they are accurate and as up-to-date as possible while reflecting your side of the story if that would be of help. For instance, if delinquent items have been paid off, it should be noted.

If, after reviewing your reports, you need to correct erroneous entries or note accounts that have been paid off or closed, request a dispute form from the agency. The process sometimes hits a snag when the creditor reporting the erroneous entry insists that it is correct. In that case, you must dispute it with the creditor rather than the credit reporting agency. If the creditor refuses to remove it, you should get busy writing your 100-word essay to file alongside the disputed entry.

Wherever the blame for the error may lie, it's your responsibility to find it and correct it. And, by all means, save your money by doing it yourself. Just this morning I saw an ad for "legal credit repair—only $99" and was reminded that, when the negative entries on your credit report are correct, there's nothing a lawyer can do that you can't do yourself, using the guidelines above.

Credit Fraud

If you puffed up your income for a mortgage application, falsified your tax returns to support a business loan application, or spent on a card you knew you couldn't pay, creditors can and may go after you for fraud.

Fortunately for you, fraud is one of the hardest causes of action to prove. To find fraud, the court must find four elements in concert with one another, including the following: the creditor must have knowledge of a material *misrepresentation* of a past or existing fact; the creditor must have *relied* on that fact; the creditor's reliance was to its *detriment*; and there has to be *intent* to induce reliance.

Right now, don't take chances. If you know in your heart of hearts you lied or if you suspect your spouse engaged in fraud, seek the help of an attorney experienced in this area of the law. You don't want to play around with fraud charges because you could land in jail and lose your children.

Also, fraudulent obligations aren't dischargeable—if proven—in bankruptcy, so there's no relief in sight from the bankruptcy courts.

One piece of protection you can use: Often creditors charge "fraud" when, in fact, legal fraud is not at issue. If a credit collection agency hounds you for unpaid bills and charges fraud, keep track of the telephone calls in a log or diary. The consumer protection laws may provide you a safe haven if collectors step overboard because they will fear that you might countersue for violation of these federal statutes.

Again, your best recourse is to see an attorney. Remember, attorney-client privilege offers you protection. Your attorney has a legally binding reason not to reveal your confidences, and attorneys can lose their licenses if they break confidences. And if your spouse engaged in fraudulent acts, in many instances, both depending on the facts and state law, you won't be legally liable.

Fraud, bankruptcy, credit crises—these are some of the unfortunate fallouts from a messy divorce, but try to hold your head up, and like Scarlett O'Hara, put on your red dress and go to the birthday party. After all, tomorrow is another day. And unless you're a celebrity, most people won't know about your problems if you don't tell them.

OTHER IMMEDIATE NEEDS

Financial emergencies such as medical crisis, job loss, business failure, and the breakdown of a car or appliances can literally do us in. Even if we have emergency funds or insurance, we can be amazed at how quickly they are eaten up or how little is covered. If we don't, it may be time for extreme measures.

CONSIDERING BANKRUPTCY

Although bankruptcy can give you a fresh start, it is not a cure-all. All forms of bankruptcy will mar your credit report for up to ten years, and all can carry harsh penalties. For instance, in Chapter 7 you will be starting over with few assets, depending on what property your state allows as exempt. Filers of Chapter 13 have complained that they felt like "indentured servants" while they completed their three- to five-year repayment plans.

The number of bankruptcies nationwide is expected to exceed 1 million for the first time ever in 1996.
—Source: American Bankruptcy Institute

What bankruptcy *can* do is get collectors off your back. All pending lawsuits must now go through the bankruptcy court. While you're in a bankruptcy program creditors cannot foreclose on your home, repossess your car, garnishee your wages, shut off your utilities, or proceed with any debt collection activities. Depending on the type of bankruptcy you file, most of your unsecured debt (such as credit cards) will be taken care of, but child support, alimony, fines, taxes, and some student loan obligations may not be excused, depending on the facts. Also dependent on the type you file and the state you live in, your secured debts such as a home or car may still not be safe after the bankruptcy proceedings are over, since you must resume payments on them in order to keep them.

The choice of whether to file and the decision about which type of protection to seek should be made in consultation with your attorney. If you do not have an attorney, choose carefully. Some lawyers use bankruptcies as "bread and butter" money, filing a large volume of cases to generate income, but doing so too quickly to consider individual needs. Although it seems unjust since you're already so far in debt, your bankruptcy filing will cost money. Lawyer fees will vary and the federal court filing fee is $160, which of course will not be excused by the bankruptcy. It is possible to find some publicly and privately-funded legal services programs who may handle your case or refer you to a private lawyer.

Avoiding Bankruptcy

As you can see, while bankruptcy is right for many, this "cure" for your financial woes can be a hard medicine to swallow. As with physical diseases, the sooner you detect your financial ailments, the greater the chance for recovery. If you catch it early enough, you may be able to handle your financial problem on your own or with the help of an agency such as Consumer Credit Counseling Service (800-388-2227), a nonprofit organization that provides free or low-cost credit counseling, help creating and sticking to a personal budget, and assistance negotiating with your creditors. But note, using this service will not protect your credit rating.

From here we go on to Part Three: The Future. We'll look at more financial steps you should be taking now in order to ensure your future prosperity and your children's well-being.

THE 7, 11, & 13'S OF BANKRUPTCY CODES

Chapter 7: Asset liquidation. Used by individuals or businesses that can't pay their debts from their income. All except "exempt" possessions (usually determined by state laws) are sold and money is divided by creditors. Provides a "fresh start," but stays on record for 10 years. Chapter 7 can only be filed every six years.

Chapter 11: Usually used to reorganize a business while the business continues to operate. Used by large corporations, but is open to both individuals and businesses with sizable debts and assets. If you are in business and facing a financial downturn, remember that today, bankruptcy must be considered to involve strategy and planning; therefore, you need to consult an attorney expert in this field so that you can come out as financially and legally unscathed as possible.

Chapter 12: Allows farmers to reorganize debts and keep their farms.

Chapter 13: Often called a "wage-earner" petition, allows people and small business owners with regular incomes to pay off all or part of their debts over a 3- to 5-year period without continuing collection measures from creditors. The upper limit for using Chapter 13 is less than $250,000 in unsecured and less than $750,000 in secured debts. (Secured debts are those in which you have pledged an asset, such as a mortgage; unsecured debts include items such as most credit and department store cards, except where you have made a major purchase such as furniture, appliances, etc.) In theory, a Chapter 13 filer can pay a very small monthly amount to satisfy the bankruptcy court requirements, although as the story below illustrates, the theory does not always work out to match the practice.

RESOURCES

Emily Card. *Staying Solvent: The Comprehensive Guide to Equal Credit for Women*. New York: Holt, Rinehart & Winston, 1985.

Emily Card. *The Ms. Money Book*. New York: E.P. Dutton, 1990.

Gerri Detweiler. *The Ultimate Credit Handbook*. New York: Penguin Books, 1993.

Emily Card's books can be ordered directly from the Women's Credit and Finance Project, PO Box 3725, Santa Monica, CA 90403. Please enclose $18 for each book plus $2 for shipping each book.

PART THREE

The Future

CHAPTER 11

Insurance: Are You Ready for Anything?

Single parents often fly with no insurance safety net because they feel they can't afford coverage, or they put their dollars into coverage that isn't tailored to their needs. This situation happens to all of us who tend to deny the possibility of a crisis on the horizon and cultivate a false sense of security that "stuff like that never happens to me." Unfortunately, this attitude is even more dangerous for the single parent because there's no other source of backup revenue. The cornerstone coverages of health, disability, and life insurance are often the only protection you can offer your children in case of your illness or death.

This chapter will help you assess your health, disability, and life insurance needs to make sure you're adequately covered without being overinsured. Other types of insurance will be addressed, as well as strategies to get the most out of your insurance dollars. Beware of some insurance agents who may not be above playing on your worst fears; selling you insurance you don't really need to make a higher commission. On the other hand, don't find yourself uninsured or underinsured when it's too late.

INSURANCE INVENTORY

Start by taking an inventory of all the policies you now have as well as those that you might be eligible for under group rates. You may be surprised by hidden policies that you weren't even aware of. Most of us think immediately of our employee benefit packages and move on to member benefits for unions, professional organizations, credit cards, bank accounts, colleges and universities, the military, and any other organization that we're members of. For example, the National Association for the Self-Employed (800-232-NASE) offers group rate insurance as one of it's membership benefits.

Like the humorous list of different ways to prepare shrimp enumerated in the 1995 movie *Forrest Gump*, there's insurance to cover any possible calamity, emergency, or fatality. Here are some insurance coverages you may already own or be the beneficiary of.

- Health insurance
- Major medical
- Hospitalization
- Disability
- Long Term Care
- Homeowner's or renter's insurance
- Earthquake insurance
- Flood insurance
- Auto insurance
- Dental insurance
- Term life insurance
- Whole life insurance
- Universal life insurance
- Variable life insurance
- Accidental death insurance
- Travel insurance
- Credit card insurance
- Umbrella insurance policies
- Liability insurance
- Errors and omissions insurance
- Professional malpractice insurances
- Crop insurance
- Special disease insurance (cancer, etc.)
- Social Security
- State disability and unemployment insurance

Note where you're duplicating or overlapping coverage and where you think you might have gaps. Duplication often happens from a combination of ignorance of what you have and what you fear you may have left unprotected. There's no easy way to see what insurance you really need. The basic rule is that you want to insure to replace both your income and assets against loss. You'll have to play the odds, knowing that you'll never be insured for all possibilities. Instead, attempt to determine the most likely calamities and hope, of course, that you'll never have to cash in on your premiums. It's a grim exercise to attend to all the terrible things that could potentially mar your life. But worse yet is to be left with nothing if fate should deal you a bad hand.

CORNERSTONE COVERAGE FOR SINGLE PARENTS

In the old days, the cornerstone of a building was it's main support. If it was pulled out, the walls would come tumbling down. Similarly, single parents should depend on health, disability, and life insurance as the cornerstones of their insurance portfolios.

Health Insurance

Virtually nonexistent only 50 years ago, health insurance is now considered a necessity and ranks among our greatest monthly expenses. Although as many as 30 percent of Americans are uninsured, don't count yourself among those numbers. At a bare minimum, you should purchase good insurance with a high deductible.

Good coverage means that after you've meet the deductible and co-insurance out-of-pocket expenses, the insurance company pays all or a large percentage of the medical bills. Healthy people should get insurance with a larger deductible because the reduction in premiums will more than make up for the larger amount initially paid if something drastic happened. People with chronic health problems should take a lower deductible.

HMOs VERSUS INDIVIDUAL PHYSICIANS

If you have good doctors, keep them and get individual insurance. If not, consider joining a health maintenance organization (HMO), but be prepared to serve as an advocate for your own case if you need referrals to specialists.

HEALTH AND DISABILITY INSURANCE: TIPS ON GETTING THE COVERAGE YOU NEED

A quick primer: A deductible is the amount you pay out of pocket before the insurance company pays a cent. The coinsurance or copayment amount is a percentage that you will still have to pay after the insurance kicks in. No matter what your deductible or coinsurance amount, you should never buy a policy without a stop-loss provision, which sets a limit on your total out of pocket spending, after which the insurance pays 100 percent of covered costs.

1. **Buy a policy with a higher yearly deductible.** The money you save in premiums will make up for the potential out-of-pocket costs you'd incur in a major disaster. Make sure you are getting a deductible that renews each year rather than for each incident. Traditionally, medical expenses incurred by any member of the family counted towards the deductible for that year. Now, insurance companies are offering policies with seemingly lower deductibles, but they do not accumulate over the year's time. In other words, you might have a $250 deductible on each single new illness or incident. If your daughter broke her arm in July, you'd pay the first $250. If your son were hospitalized for an asthma attack in October, you'd start over with another $250 deductible rather than having what you paid earlier count towards this one.

2. **Choose the longest waiting period you can stand** before your disability or long-term care (for an extensive illness) benefits kick in, although I don't recommend over a 90-day waiting period. Remember, you'll be out of the work force for that 90 days, so consider what resources would get you through until your policy kicks in.

3. **Never buy a policy without a stop-loss clause.** This important clause may add more expense to your premiums, but it's better to cut corners in other areas. After all, the amount you'd be paying up front in terms of a higher deductible or higher co-insurance percentage would be a drop in the bucket compared to what you'd have to pay as your medical expenses mounted with no stop-loss.

4. **Try to avoid lifetime benefit caps.** Although about 70 percent of health insurance policies have a lifetime cap (typically about $1 million), in a real catastrophe you could use up your lifetime allotment in a matter of years and be left at the mercy of government programs such as Medicaid. Look for a policy that forgoes the lifetime cap and support legislative efforts being lobbied by Christopher Reeve, an actor who became paralyzed from the neck down in a 1995 accident, that would require a $10 million minimum for lifetime caps.

5. **Don't forget long-term care insurance.** While Americans can expect longer life spans and the cost of health care continues to rise, few people will consider buying long-term care policies. Consider, though, that the average cost of a nursing home in the U.S. is $25,000 to $30,000 annually and 70% of single people who enter a nursing home become impoverished within a year. Currently, Medicare only pays about 2% of long-term care costs, and with Federal cutbacks, you should not expect Medicaid to fill in the gap. While nursing home days may seem far off to many, single parents in their middle years or those with elderly parents should think about whether long-term care insurance is necessary. Current policies vary dramatically, but in general, you should look for a policy that would cover you for at least three years with an adequate daily benefit (about $150).

Choices about health insurance can be very complex. In fact, policies differ so dramatically that it's almost impossible to compare them item by item. To narrow the playing field, start by deciding the amount of the deductible, then compare rates for group versus individual coverage. In most cases, with a group (unless it's a high-risk group such as construction workers, etc.), you'll get better rates because the insurance company is "diluting" the mix of healthy and sick people with many individuals, so enough healthy people pay premiums to make up for the expenses of the sick ones.

The next choice you'll make is between family coverage and individual coverage for each family member. This choice is a stinker for the single parent because family coverage still tends to be biased toward a traditional family model with one earner and several dependents (including spouse and children). These policies work best for those with several children because the premiums are often the same no matter how many dependents are claimed. Other single parents will find it more economical to purchase individual policies for each family member, taking advantage of the group rates for which they might be eligible. Older, well children can be covered by school insurance. Of course, children with congenital health problems will be more challenging to cover. Check policies in your area.

Disability Insurance

Most people erroneously worry about getting life insurance, but in reality they're much more likely to become disabled than to die by accident when their children are young. Although your health or life policies you may have through work may have a disability rider, you're probably not well enough protected. The majority of disability policies don't even start payment until someone has been sick for 60 days, when statistically he or she probably would have recovered anyway. Of course, shorter time limits will increase premiums, so you need to find a balance.

Disability coverage is especially important for the self-employed or for people who believe they might have health problems down the line. Consider purchasing private disability insurance even when it's available through your employer. In these times when jobs are so uncertain, insurance that you have to qualify for such as disability coverage may be hard to pick up again if it lapses while you change jobs. If not, group insurance might give you a minimal policy that you don't have to qualify for, but at least it will give you a thread to hang onto in a worst-case scenario.

Speaking of worst-case scenarios, the length of time the company will have to pay benefits is another variable that affects the cost. If you can afford it, purchase a policy that would cover you until age 65, when your Social Security benefits kick in. At the very least, purchase three years' worth of coverage to give you time to get back on your feet.

Conventional wisdom shows that mortgage disability insurance is not a good investment because the odds are you won't use it. However, it may be a good deal for the peace of mind. The benefit is paid monthly, and because you usually don't have to qualify, the actual dollar cost is low and the stakes are high.

A final word about disability coverage. A policy that covers you when you can't work in any occupation may seem like better coverage. Yet by buying a policy that covers you when you're not able to do your *own* job, you may be able to earn a small income by doing something else to supplement your disability payments, without the threat of losing that needed income. A teacher had to sit out of work for an entire year while he healed from a nearly fatal car accident. But from his hospital bed and later his own home, he was able to supplement his disability payments with consulting work for clients with special needs children. Since his disability insurance covered only his specific teaching job, he was free to pursue the less strenuous job without losing his benefits.

Life Insurance

Term or whole (permanent)? That is the question. While experts have their pet reasons for preferring one over the other, here I maintain that it's a question of circumstance. Term insurance is less expensive for the same death benefit as whole or universal life, but it does not build capital or equity for you. Permanent (i.e.whole or universal life) policies all have value you can borrow against.

It's the difference between renting an apartment and buying a home. You get the same space (or amount of coverage), but while rent may be cheaper, you're throwing the money down the drain. Owning a home is probably more expensive, but your payoff is the amount of equity you build that you can either borrow against or cash in by selling.

To strike a balance, the industry has created a type of whole life coverage called universal life. The policy allows greater flexibility than whole life or term by letting you vary throughout your life how long you want the death benefit to be in effect, how long you will pay premiums, and how much cash value you want to accumulate. The policy also gives you the flexibility throughout your life to raise or lower premiums and raise or lower the death benefit. Your choices determine your premiums. Although the policy's first year premium is more than that for term insurance, your ability to vary premium and death benefit and to build cash makes the policy an attractive alternative. However, if you're not careful about paying enough money, the policy will lapse. In addition, such policies are interest sensitive. As interest rates go down, your policy terms may be extended. Keep track by getting—and reading—your yearly report.

Be cautious about variable life—a newer type of policy—where you get to choose investment options for your premium. These policies

> ### TAKING THE PULSE OF YOUR LIFE INSURANCE POLICY
>
> Request a disclosure document called an in-force policy ledger, which shows the current cash value of your policy and projects how much cash the policy should accumulate over time.

provide life insurance along with investment options but may not be appropriate, depending on your financial circumstances.

If you're going to need insurance for a long time, such as if you have a two-year-old, whole life or universal life may be a good idea after all. Or, you may start out with a combination of term and permanent insurance. Then, slowly phase out the term coverage as the premiums rise in the future. (Permanent insurance premiums are generally more expensive initially but drop as the policy builds value.)

Again, it's worth underscoring that you should look into getting insurance through some group you're already in. Most single parents' biggest worry is what would happen if they die and their kids are left without any income. If you have any health problems or feel you might be hard to cover, combine two or three different smaller policies as they're offered through group automatic coverage.

ESTIMATING YOUR LIFE INSURANCE NEEDS

1. How many years do you want to provide income to your family?   _____
2. How much will they need per year?   _____
3. Multiply line 1 by line 2.   _____
4. How much will you set aside for burial costs?   _____
5. What are your projected probate or trust expenses?   _____
6. Add lines 3, 4, and 5.   _____
7. What are your total current assets, not counting your home, less your liabilities?   _____
8. Subtract line 7 from line 6.   _____

The amount in line 8 is the face value of the life insurance policy you need now to provide for your dependents and keep your other assets intact. This chart assumes no inflation and that the insurance proceeds will be exhausted at the end of the term.

ADDITIONAL COVERAGE YOU'LL PROBABLY NEED

Any coverage you can possibly think of is already out there waiting to be bought. But there are certain policies that most of us take for granted: automobile insurance, because it's mandated by law in most states, and homeowner's insurance, because it's usually tied up in our mortgage payments in an escrow account, so we practically forget about it.

Automobile Insurance

One nice thing about being single is that somebody else's driving record can't muddy your own premiums. Single parent Malone Lindsey recalls her first shock as a newlywed when her car insurance went up because of her husband's DUI. She realized she was tied to this man "for better or for worse." But it got worse than that, so she eventually got out.

The primary choice for Malone and all of us is whether we need liability (covers the damage you do to others) or collision (covers the damage you or somebody else does to your own car) insurance and in what amounts. Most states require a minimum amount of liability insurance. You may want to carry more in case you're in an accident with a high-value vehicle. A $25,000 policy may seem like a lot if you're driving a clunker, but it won't go very far if you rear-end a Lexus. The same goes for medical liability. The state's minimum doesn't consider the high medical costs and potential for lawsuits. You have more leeway with your collision coverage, and it's up to you to decide whether you'll gamble. Collision rates can be so high that some people actually base their car-buying decisions on the costs of the premiums, driving their agents crazy with numerous calls to look up certain makes and models (by the way, you should do this if you're car shopping. That's what the agent is there for). If you're borrowing money to buy your car, the lender can require a certain amount of coverage. Collision insurance is a good idea especially if you buy or lease an expensive car.

> Comparison shop for insurance over the phone: Try GEICO (800-841-3000), Progressive (800-288-6776), and State Farm (check local listing).

Homeowner's Policy or Renter's Insurance

Renters have lost everything in a fire only to discover that their landlord's homeowner's policy didn't cover any of the contents of their home. This mistake could wipe us out at a time when we're already vulnerable. A simple version of a homeowner's policy called renter's insurance could have helped ease the transition. After taking inventory of your home, you determine an approximate value for your goods and purchase a policy. It's even possible to carry riders for natural disasters such as hurricanes, tornadoes, floods, or earthquakes on your renter's insurance. Depending on the area, you should look into the appropriate coverage.

A regular homeowner's policy covers the land, home, and contents as well as medical liability for accidents on the property. For both renter's and homeowner's policies, be sure to buy the option that increases coverage to replacement cost of home and contents rather than only the actual value. In other words, if your TV is stolen, you should get the amount of money it would take to purchase a new TV, not the amount that your old TV was worth. Depreciation is usually figured by the age of an item, so you could really lose money on electronics, appliances, and computer equipment unless you get replacement cost insurance.

Make sure your renter's or homeowner's policy also contains a general liability *umbrella* clause to protect you in case of lawsuits that arise from accidents on your property.

DEALING WITH THE AGENTS

Just as we rely on a good travel agent to put all the pieces of our trip together, a reliable insurance agent can save you trouble and get you a better price if you carry several policies through the same agency. It's definitely less confusing in your time of need when you know exactly who to turn to. Find out whether the agents work on commission, and always go with your gut feelings.

As you and your agent develop a long-standing relationship, your agent will become a helpful commodity. By becoming acquainted with your circumstances, your agent will better project your insurance needs. For instance, your homeowner's policy may require extra riders to cover expensive computer equipment. If you happen to mention your recent computer upgrade to a good agent, the agent will be sure to remind you to upgrade your insurance as well. You can also call on this agent for special favors, such as issuing you a binder over the phone when you purchase a new vehicle.

While this person will become a valuable asset and perhaps even a good friend, keep in mind that an insurance agent isn't a financial planner. Choose only objective third parties for your financial planning needs. Insurance agents are too close to the situation with the promise of sales commissions possibly clouding their judgment. Beware especially of insurance salespersons posing as financial planners who offer to help you plan your estate (more on this in Chapter 14).

Your dealings with the company should be above reproof. If you follow all their protocols to a "T," they'll have more reason to take you seriously. You should be professional and assertive with company representatives with whom you come into contact. Create a paper trail of all your dealings, from saving receipts, policies, and company literature to taking the extra trouble to make copies of all the forms you send in or letters you write. While telephone negotiations can be useful, they're harder to document. Be sure to take accurate notes of the time and date, name and title of your contact(s), and the results of your call.

If you feel that you're being treated unfairly, recall the young lawyer in John Grisham's novel *The Rainmaker* who went up against his downtrodden client's negligent insurance company, finding that, "They prey on the uneducated, and when claims are made on the policies the companies routinely turn them down."

Whether this is an accurate representation of the insurance industry or not, it certainly rings true to many who go up against such industry giants with their meager resources. To avoid an all-out court battle, make your appeals through the appropriate channels, first internally within the company, then through arbitration, with court as a last resort.

Internally, move up the chain of command to level letters of complaint against supervisors. As with the original claims form, keep your facts straight and your delivery neat and precise. If you think the adjuster has been negligent in some way, such as by failing to treat your case promptly or follow proper procedures, point this out. Remember, you're hoping that each step you make will be the one that solves the standoff, but you never know if it's just another step in the road toward court. Do yourself a favor by documenting every step you make, whether it's a meeting with the company executive or a simple phone call to check on your claim.

MAKING CLAIMS

As you probably noticed if you read the fine print when you were shopping for coverage, policies are written in a way that minimizes the companies' losses. The same is true for the filing procedures. If you don't follow them carefully (and they will vary from company to company), you may lose some or all of your benefits.

Steps to Take

It is best to familiarize yourself with the claim procedures ahead of time in case you ever need to use them. Generally, you will encounter the following chain of events:

1. **You notify the insurance company.** Pay special attention to time limits (e.g., thirty days from the initial incident), the way in which you are required to notify (by phone, in writing, etc.), and whom you should notify (a specific phone number or address).

2. **You file a formal claim.** Request copies of claim forms when you first sign up with a company. If you know before an accident ever happens what questions might be asked later on, you're more likely to pay attention to important details while you're still on the scene.

3. **The insurance company assigns an adjuster and your case is investigated.** The adjuster will routinely look for legal ways to deny your claim. If you were behind on your premiums or if your policy contained an exemption to the condition you're filing for, your claim may be rejected outright. If your valid claim makes it through this first round, the next step is to verify the assertions you've made. The adjuster may ask you for receipts for stolen goods, death certificates for life insurance claims, or official documents like police reports to check the circumstances surrounding an accident. Finally, once the facts are taken into account, the investigation will move to a more subtle playing field. The adjuster will determine whether you (the insured) acted in such a way to worsen the damages and may investigate further about the value of the claimed loss.

4. **The adjuster makes a recommendation to the company.** Based on findings from the investigation, the adjuster may notify the company that your claim should be honored (and in what amount), that it should be resisted, or a combination of the two. If the recommendation includes partial or total payment of the claim, the adjuster will ask you for your signature on a proof-of-loss form to forward to the company.

5. **The company makes a decision based on the adjuster's report and notifies you in writing through the mail.**

6. **The insurance company carries out the award.** Depending on the circumstances, this could include a direct payment to you or indirect payment through defending you in court, etc. *Warning: Before cashing an insurance settlement check, consider that your signature on the check indicates that you legally accept the payment as payment in full, unless you can prove that you were forced or misled into signing it.*

7. **You agree or disagree with the award.** Whether it's as much as you wanted or not, you can always agree to take what the company offers you. But if you've read the steps in this box or been through a claims procedure in real life, you know that there are plenty of opportunities for a disagreement to arise with the company that's supposed to be protecting you in your time of loss. If you decide to challenge the company's decision, you could be in for a real struggle, setting yourself up as a David to the company's Goliath.

If a person-to-person meeting is called for, be prepared as if you were going to court. Take all documents pertaining to your case, and memorize the steps you've taken and the reason you're right. Know ahead of time where you're willing to compromise but, of course, don't advertise that you will. In making that decision, you'll be factoring in the trouble you've taken, the likelihood that you'd be able to get more than you're being offered, and the type of justice involved. In *The Rainmaker*, the mother whose son died because the company didn't pay for his treatment didn't care how much money she got; she just wanted the company to admit they were wrong in public.

If you're dealing with a potentially large sum, you should bring an attorney to the meeting or at least consult one before you go to both familiarize yourself with your legal rights and help determine if you have any holes in your argument. Afterward, send a letter of confirmation outlining your perspective of the meeting's results. A courteous and prompt follow-up will demonstrate that you've really got your act together.

If you must move to arbitration, realize that although it will be more informal and less expensive than going to court, you're still looking at an expensive proposition. Typically, you and the company must each pay for your own arbitrator and must split the cost of a third one. You may even need your attorney to be present in complex cases.

Arbitration guidelines may be specified in your policy and may vary by state. Check to see whether they're binding or nonbinding before you agree to the procedure. If you're turned down in a binding arbitration, you can still choose to appeal in court, though your chances of success will be greatly reduced.

Take a proactive stance early on by filing promptly and through the correct channels. If you've done your part correctly but still haven't received the benefits you feel you deserve, you may be forced to file a lawsuit for breach of contract and/or bad faith. This area of the law is rapidly evolving and extends beyond the scope of this book, but if you think you've got a case you should report your company to your state's insurance department and consult the resources below for more information on how to fight it.

While insurance gives you a security net in case of factors beyond your control, a college education provides a different kind of security for you and your children. Read on to find out how to make your educational dreams possible for yourself and your children.

RESOURCES

John Grisham. *The Rainmaker.* New York: Island Books, 1995.

Donald J. Korn. *Your Money or Your Life: How to Save Thousands on Your Health Care Insurance.* New York: Collier/Macmillan, 1992.

Ralph Nader and Wesley J. Smith. *Winning the Insurance Game: The Complete Consumer's Guide to Saving Money, Revised Edition.* NY: Doubleday, 1993.

William M. Shernoff and Thelma O'Brian. *Payment Refused: A Crusading Lawyer's Dramatic Cases Against Insurance Companies.* New York: Richardson and Steirman, 1986.

CHAPTER 12

Planning for College

Although many failed couples are too bitter to plan together, if at all possible, you need to include your former spouse in college planning early. Don't let yourself be distracted by old grievances. Focusing on what's best for your mutual offspring can make it a positive and fruitful experience. One divorced couple with two children has a tradition of purchasing savings bonds earmarked for college each year on their children's birthdays and again at the winter holidays. Each parent buys whatever denomination he or she can afford at the time. Additionally, they spread the word around their extended families that money gifts go into a special savings account for college unless the giver specifies otherwise. Although they haven't saved a fortune this way, their actions point toward an important college planning objective: Set the expectation early that children will attend college and keep periodic attention focused on this goal. By raising family consciousness on this matter, they encourage help from gift givers as well, who will typically contribute to the college fund in addition to regular gifts.

If there is no other parent in the picture because of death, adoption, or disappearance, you needn't go it alone. As in the aforementioned example, enlist the help of anyone who's willing to lend a sympathetic ear. Become a champion of your cause. Along with the usual help from friends and relatives, don't overlook your child's guidance counselor at school.

With such a high student-to-counselor ratio, it's often true that the "squeaky wheel" gets all the attention. Whether or not your child is already a squeaky wheel, your guidance counselor is an excellent source to tap on the road to college. He or she can tell you about getting ready for tests such as the SAT and ACT, selecting and applying for schools, financial aid, scholarships, and grants.

Research: Get information on ACT/SAT testing courses; do they have a higher success rate? Tips on acing the tests. A $500 investment in the course might yield a full scholarship that could be worth thousands.

ENSURING A BRIGHT FUTURE

Studies show that only 50 percent of our young people are going on to higher education. Yet according to the 1996 Economic Report of the President, each year of formal education after high school adds 5 to 15% to a worker's annual earnings later on. Other Census data support the fact that college is the key to higher earnings and an enhanced quality of life. Whereas attending college can't necessarily promise these things, it can tilt the balance in your child's favor.

Savings Options: What Will Work for You?

The classic advice on saving for college goes something like this: Figure out which years your child will be attending college. Then find those years on the American Association of Colleges and Universities chart that projects how much it will cost you. After being revived from your shock-induced fainting spell, you can then decide how much you need to be putting away weekly to reach these goals. Depending on the age of your child and the choice of college, you might find that this is more than you're spending on groceries for the entire family. Multiply by more than one child, and you're sure to feel overwhelmed by this monumental task. Don't despair. Options do exist.

Ways to Do It

Like other families discussed in this chapter, you can tailor savings methods to your own situation. Use the following tips alone or together to get the job done.

- Put aside money weekly, monthly, or yearly even if it's not as much as the charts recommend.

- Require your child to put a percentage of his or her allowance into a college fund.

- Take on a couple of special projects early, put money in the bank, and let compound interest work for you.

- Require working teens to put aside a certain amount for college as a condition for allowing them to work.

Places to Put It

Your children's college fund will become your family's sacred cow. Don't touch it. If you're afraid that your willpower won't hold, find a savings vehicle that will grow your sacred cow and make it impossible (or mighty difficult) for you to "butcher" it. Additionally, consider whether your savings vehicle will double as a tax shelter.

Standard savings account: Good as a starter, but way too easy to dip into when the going gets tough. Typically these earn about four percent and will help keep your money's value in the face of inflation.

Savings bonds: The traditional college standby can still work, but changes in the Treasury laws have lowered your potential return. One plus: if you meet certain income guidelines and use your bonds to pay for college, you may be able to forgo paying federal income tax on them.

Mutual fund: Provides an easy way to get a higher return without as much risk as playing the stock market. Look for a mutual fund that encourages college savings by allowing smaller investments (such as $50 monthly) and easier payment methods (electronic funds transfer straight from your bank account). Remember, though, equity and bond funds fluctuate with the markets.

DETERMINATION

In 1968, Frances Peters found herself divorced with custody of her seven-year-old daughter. Determined to see her daughter achieve a college education, she started a cottage industry in her home, overseeing six full-time seamstresses in addition to her regular job. Today, her daughter has a medical degree. Frances counsels that as a single parent, "you still have a responsibility of raising a child with all options open. You're still a family. A whole family."

TAKING THE BITE OUT: REDUCING COLLEGE COSTS

In-State Tuition: If your child's college of choice is a state school in another state, consider establishing residency in that state. Save about 50% over the life of a four-year degree and even more if your child continues for graduate-level work.

Once you've enrolled as an out-of-state student, most schools won't let you switch over to in-state tuition unless you are a permanent resident. But if allowed, you should do it as soon as possible.

Faculty and Staff Discounts: Schools offer dramatic discounts to faculty and staff and their children. Some even offer free tuition. This benefit, potentially valued at thousands each year, could be worth changing jobs for. "Double Trouble" families will benefit the most from this discount, since both the parents and their offspring can take advantage.

If the noncustodial parent is working at a university, your children might still be eligible for benefits. Check it out.

Living Arrangements: There are pros and cons for every type of living arrangement, but in pure economic terms living at home can't be beat. If the choice is between no college at all or living at home and attending the local college, there's no shame in the latter choice.

For those who are going away to school, weigh carefully the options of dorm versus apartment living. Many schools require freshmen to live in a dorm and buy a food plan. This was the case for my niece, Jennifer but she and her roommate quickly figured out that the amounts they were jointly paying for the dorm and food plan could easily support them in an apartment.

Transportation: Vehicles are expensive. After paying insurance, bank notes, and repairs, there may be nothing left for gas money! If the student will be living on campus and not holding down an outside job, consider public transportation or a bicycle viable options.

Hidden Expenses: Many classes have hidden expenses that could drain hundreds of dollars from your wallet. Before registering for art or lab-type classes, find out if supplies are included in tuition. You may need to put these courses off if they're not essential at the moment.

Tuition Ceilings: Typically, a certain amount of tuition is charged per semester hour earned, up to a "ceiling," which is the flat rate paid for full-time tuition. Most colleges consider 12 semester hours to be full-time enrollment, but they'll allow students to enroll in more classes (up to about 19 hours) without paying any additional tuition.

If 18 credit hours seems like a tough academic load, remember that the amount you "save" on tuition this way may mean that your child will have to work less on outside jobs and will graduate sooner.

Greek Life: Sorry, there's just no getting around the high expense of sororities and fraternities. If you have strong affiliations with one, you'll have to make financial sacrifices elsewhere to enable this goal. An alternative? Encourage your student to get involved with another group, such as a campus religious organization, student council, activities council, intramural sports, or clubs associated with favorite hobbies.

Trust funds: For the serious college planner. Depending on the type of fund, it may be virtually impossible to access this money until college. Can provide a tax shelter and a way for grandparents to transfer wealth. *Managing Your Inheritance* provides a complete overview of trusts. As mentioned in Chapter 2, your marital dissolution agreement can be set up to require your Ex to start and fund an educational trust. Consult your accountant and/or lawyer to decide what's best in your situation.

Individual school savings plan: A fad of the eighties, when college costs soared while government help declined, these plans locked parents into a specific school or state system by allowing them to prepay at today's tuition rates. Several states still offer them, but I don't recommend them for the simple reason that you just can't predict what your child will do that far in advance. Even if you get a refund later, you will have tied up your money for many years with no investment returns. "A nice way for the parent to save, but a serious gamble," says Jay Bragdon of Conservest Management Company in Boston.

FREE ADVICE

Call 800-4-FED-AID (800-433-3243) or write to Federal Student Aid Information Center, P. O. Box 84, Washington, D.C. 20044-0084 for an excellent and comprehensive booklet on the student aid programs you might be eligible for. Ask for *The Student Guide: Financial Aid from the U.S. Department of Education, 1996-97* (or the upcoming school year). The hearing impaired may call a toll-free TDD line: 800-730-8913.

ALTERNATIVE SOURCES OF FUNDING

Scholarships, grants, and loans are out there. It's up to you to decide which ones you might be eligible for and to go after them. Additionally, you and your child should come to an early understanding about the amount of money the child will be expected to contribute to the funding of his or her own education.

University scholarship offices often have files and files full of private scholarships ranging from $50 and up that languish without getting awarded because nobody knows to apply for them. It is up to the individual scholarships to choose their recipients. Many are generally academic or community service-type scholarships with variable requirements. One savvy student combined six such scholarships with student loans to make it through college.

The *Worldwide College Scholarship Directory* lists over 1,000 undergraduate scholarships, grants, and awards available in the U.S. and another 500 available in 75 countries around the world.

Career Press, Box 687, Dept. RF, Franklin Lakes, NJ 07417 ($19.99), 800-227-3371.

GENERAL UNIVERSITY SCHOLARSHIPS

Planning ahead is crucial here. Start making inquiries early in your child's junior year of high school. The earlier you and your child make the decision about where to go to school, the better. In fact, sixty percent of Ivy League slots were filled by early admission for fall of 1996.

You must get your general admission application in and be accepted to the university before you will be considered for scholarships. The earlier you make your decision, the more lead time to contact the general scholarship office and find out about the variety of scholarships and requirements needed to get them. Don't think in terms of getting your paperwork in by the deadline and fall into the trap of rushing to the post office to get it postmarked on time. One frantic family actually drove to the postmaster's house before midnight and asked him to postmark their application. Luckily, it was a small town and he was glad to oblige. But this kind of thinking is not what gets you the prime scholarships. Case in point: The same family that rushed to the post office ended up getting the four-year tuition scholarship for their daughter, but if they had turned in the same exact application three months earlier, they could have gotten book stipends worth an additional $1,600 over the life of the scholarship. Following is a sampling of typical university offerings and what you can expect from each one.

- **Academic:** Based on minimum ACT/SAT scores and GPA requirements, then student involvement in extracurricular activities is used to narrow the field.

- **Adult:** Some universities offer help for adults that showed merit in high school and afterward show work or other credentials that indicate a commitment to education. Use for your older children that haven't yet attended college, or for yourself.

- **Alumni:** If you have friends or relatives who were alumni, your child may be eligible.

- **Departmental:** Check with the college of your major for special scholarship opportunities. This source is especially important for graduate students.

- **Minority:** Despite bad press for affirmative action and "quotas," universities use minority scholarships as a tool to bolster their multicultural array.

- **Sports:** If your child is a candidate for a sports scholarship, you've probably dealt with recruiters and the like already.

GOVERNMENT GRANTS

Where else can you spend three hours filling out some paperwork and come away with thousands of dollars for your effort? Certainly, Pell grants have suffered severe blows with government cutbacks, but for many, they're still practically a sure bet. Single parents alert: Pell applications are based on information from your tax forms, which will be more complicated because you're a single parent. Alert #2: Grant money that's left after tuition is paid is considered taxable income.

Unfortunately, there will be some families that make just a little too much money to get the grants, yet don't have enough to fund their children's educations. Or they may receive an award that seems like a pittance in the face of the huge costs of higher education. These folks should turn toward other options, with special attention to loans.

STUDENT LOANS

Your student loan will be funded by one of two sources. If it comes directly from the government via your school, it is under the Federal Direct Student Loan Program (Direct Loan). If it comes through a private lender but is guaranteed by the federal government, it is a Federal Family Education Loan (FFEL). The source of your funds will depend on which program(s) your school participates in. Under either program your school determines your eligibility and disperses the funds. Following is a list of the types of loans available. As you will see, their names vary slightly according to which main program they're under, but the terms are almost identical.

Stafford Loans are paid back by students and have a variable interest rate that under current law will not exceed 8.25%. Repayment does not begin until a grace period of six months after the student graduates, leaves school, or drops below half-time enrollment. Applicants with greater financial need will receive subsidized Stafford Loans in which the federal government pays interest until repayment begins and during authorized periods of deferment (such as returning to school) later on. Applicants who receive unsubsidized Stafford loans must repay their own

THE GREAT PAPER CHASE: APPLYING FOR FINANCIAL AID

1. Call or visit the university's financial-aid office to obtain the initial paperwork, which normally includes the school's financial-aid application, an extensive form from an independent agency such as ACT (different than the ACT test; it's a financial survey) or the Free Application for Federal Student Aid that will be analyzed and reported to the school, and a separate loan application from each loan program.

2. Determine the deadlines for each piece of paperwork. Some will be dependent on your tax forms, so you'll have to get your taxes done early to meet the financial-aid deadlines.

3. Find out whether the noncustodial parent will need to complete any paperwork and let him or her know as soon as possible.

4. Get to know your financial-aid officer in person. That way, if there are any problems getting paperwork from the missing parent, he or she will be sympathetic.

5. Keep two photocopies of all paperwork. If they lose one, you'll have one to send them and one for your records. Believe me, it happens.

6. Get the paperwork in before the deadlines.

7. Be proactive: track the progress. Call to find out if they have everything they need on file at the appropriate times. Find out when they'll be able to tell you something.

8. Remember, there will be at least three separate offices you'll deal with at the university: admissions, financial aid, and scholarships. Don't assume that they share paperwork or know anything about one another. Especially with large universities, it's your responsibility to find out when the paperwork is due in to each office and to get it in on time.

interest as it accrues or allow it to "capitalize" (be added to the principle of the loan). Capitalizing the interest increases the overall repayment amount, but it reduces the immediate financial burden. The amount a student can borrow depends on financial need, years in school, years left to complete the program, and whether the parent was eligible for a PLUS loan.

PLUS loans are available to parents who can either pass a credit check or obtain a co-signer who can pass the credit check. Parents can borrow a yearly limit that is equal to the student's cost of attendance minus any other financial aid for which the student is eligible. The interest rate is variable, but it will never exceed nine percent. Unlike the

Stafford Loan, repayment must begin almost immediately—60 days after the final loan disbursement is made. Interest begins to accumulate at the time of the first disbursement and is not subsidized by the federal government. Under certain circumstances, parents may apply for a deferment (no payments for a period of time, though interest still accrues) or a forbearance (reduced payments for a period of time) under certain conditions. A student may also obtain repayment assistance for the parent by serving in the military.

Consolidation loans are also available to combine several student loans into one monthly payment or to renegotiate the repayment terms of a single loan. Varieties include subsidized, unsubsidized, and PLUS consolidation loans.

Federal Perkins Loans are for students (graduate or undergraduate) with exceptional need and currently carry a lower interest rate of five percent. Loan origination and insurance fees common to the above programs are all waived, although late charges and collection costs still apply if you are negligent about repayment. Repayment terms are also more lenient, with a nine- (as opposed to six) month grace period and up to ten years to pay it off. Interest is subsidized as with the Stafford Loan, above.

THE STUDENT'S CONTRIBUTION

Help your child take college seriously by asking the student to contribute in some way. At a minimum, give your child some responsibility with getting the paperwork in by the deadlines. Many families have an understanding that the student will contribute financially by working. Guide your child into a job experience that will benefit him or her in the long run as well as supplement financial needs.

Work-Study Programs

Work-study programs aren't lucrative, but they keep your child on campus and in a supervised situation. Additionally, your child can pick up valuable skills as well as learn about the inner workings of the university. For instance, one student got a job in the library and was even able to study "on the clock" when his job duties were completed. He learned data entry and filing skills and made many good contacts in the university administration that benefited him later as he was entering the job market. Apply for work-study by checking the appropriate box on the general financial-aid application. There is not a choice at first about where your child is placed, but once a student is accepted, a transfer to a position that is closer to his or her field of study can be requested.

Off-Campus Jobs

If your child is staying in town to go to school, he or she may continue with a job held down in high school. Some parents encourage jobs only during school vacations, to avoid interference with academic pursuits. Others feel that keeping a regular work schedule during school teaches the student to budget time wisely and may take some focus away from partying. Either way, look for jobs that are flexible, part-time, and close to campus. And while pay is important now for survival, weigh carefully the hidden benefits of a job more closely related to the child's field of study even if it doesn't pay as much. If you're in a better position financially, ask your child to schedule a couple of hours each week in a volunteer organization. Whether your child gets paid or not, he or she learns real-life skills and a valuable sense of responsibility.

56 percent of full-time students hold down a job.
—Source: The Interep Radio Store

DOUBLE TROUBLE: WHEN YOU'RE BOTH IN SCHOOL

Although sending yourself and your family through school at the same time is not a task for the weak at heart, it's a winning investment in your family's welfare. We saw earlier the effects of higher education on quality of life, but you should note the special rewards for an adult that goes back for career renewal, as a beginning to a new life.

Adult Student Development Office

If your school has such a department, they're surely aware of the trends of adults returning to education. These departments can be invaluable in walking you through the paperwork and finding programs to match your needs. Take full advantage by asking for the list of adult-oriented, for-credit classes such as how to use the university library, night classes, or extended three-hour classes held only once a week to save trips to campus.

Career Services

Once enrolled, you'll have access to career counseling and guidance services: Use them. Inquire about testing to help you determine what careers match your interests. Later, you should frequent the placement office. Take advantage of seminars on filling out job applications and interviewing. Read the bulletin boards regularly for job openings. This advice is applicable to your child as well.

Student Housing

Though quality varies dramatically at different schools, adult student family housing can be a real bargain. For example, the University of Memphis offers 1- to 3-bedroom townhouses and flats in a secluded parklike setting for only $375 to $450 per month. It's a haven for single parents, who have built a loose support network for carpooling, baby-sitting, and meals.

If you're starting college planning for your infant, bravo. But if you've waited until your child is a high school senior, don't beat yourself up. This is not a perfect world. Take what you can use in this chapter and run with it. Believe it or not, your child will thank you one day. And you will thank yourself.

GETTING THE MOST FOR YOUR MONEY

Books and classes are just one part of the college experience. A student activity fee is built into tuition amounts whether you use the college perks or not. Your ID card will typically get you discounts all over town, from movie tickets to public parks admissions. You may be able to attend school lectures, art events, theater, and of course, sports functions for free.

Of course, more serious services are available as well. For instance, group or individual personal counseling may be available free to students and their families. This perk alone could be a tremendous asset to a family grieving the missing parent. And by all means, don't overlook the departmental study help centers, where you or your child can get free tutoring from departmental interns and graduate assistants.

RESOURCES

Daniel Cassidy. *The Scholarship Book*. Englewood Cliffs, NJ: Prentice Hall, 1993.

Daniel Cassidy. *Worldwide College Scholarship Directory*. 4th ed.. Franklin Lakes, NJ: Career Press, 1995.

Martin M. Shenkman. *The Complete Book of Trusts*. New York: John Wiley & Sons.

Charles Shields. *The College Guide for Parents*. Chicago: Surrey Books, 1986.

O'Neal Turner with John Pivovarnick. *The Complete Idiot's Guide to Getting into College*. Alpha Books, 1994.

CHAPTER 13

Retirement Security

You must provide for your own retirement. Don't assume that you can depend on your former spouse, Uncle Sam, or even your company's pension plan. Instead, build your own three pillars of financial security.

The three basic components of a secure retirement are Social Security benefits; home ownership or rent replacement strategies; and a retirement plan such as a pension or IRA. Most of us must rely on a combination of these to provide an adequate lifestyle for the approximately one-third of our lives we will spend in retirement.

"Not many people ever look back and say, 'Darn, I saved too much for retirement.'"
—1996 ADVERTISEMENT

Unfortunately, statistics suggest that few single parents in particular have adequate retirement plans. As we live longer, it seems impossible that Social Security benefits can hold out for the duration. As they stand, their amounts would be almost impossible to live on without some supplemental help. Single parents also have a lower incidence of home ownership. In a divorce, only one person gets to keep the house, or it may have been liquidated to divide the assets equally, leaving neither parent with the benefit of home ownership. Once displaced, single parents have a harder time getting mortgage loans in their new financial reality. Most single parents who head households remain renters. Finally, although women make up the majority of single parents, only 21.5 percent of women are entitled to any kind of pension, compared with 45.2 percent of men. Of all taxpayers, in 1986, only 15 percent had opened an IRA; with tax reform and accompanying changes in eligibility rules, the number dropped to 6.8 percent in 1987.

REALITIES VERSUS ASSUMPTIONS

The realities of longer life spans, shrinking Social Security reserves, and healthier senior populations are changing our retirement assumptions from those of the previous generation. A recent article in *Parade* magazine featured a number of centenarians, noting that seniors that make it past their late 70s and beyond are not necessarily the drain on our medical resources that has been claimed. In fact, they're not the ones who are having the expensive surgeries. Those folks requiring massive operations are probably not living to be quite so old. Although medical expenses will be higher because of sheer volume, the real concern for those with longer life spans is basic living expenses—clothing, shelter, and if they're lucky, transportation.

How will your lifestyle change as you raise your children and emerge into retirement. I hope you've got an idea of what you want to be doing from your goal setting in Chapter 4. Focus more specifically on the retirement years by asking yourself the following questions:

- How do I envision my own retirement?
- Will I work? Part-time? Full-time?
- Where will I live? Will I relocate?
- How much money will I need to maintain my accustomed standard of living?
- Who will take care of me if I become ill?

You must consider your exact financial needs and goals before you can set savings goal for retirement plans.

THE FIRST PILLAR: SOCIAL SECURITY BENEFITS

If you will receive Social Security benefits for retirement, the income will not be sufficient to live on, but it offers support to the other two retirement pillars. Your benefit level as an individual retiree will be calculated based on your earnings and the number of years you've been employed.

If you're divorced after having been married for 10 years or more, you're entitled to draw on your former spouse's account (formerly, 20 years of marriage were required). If you have earned your own Social Security through employment, you have a choice of the higher benefits—your own or half your former spouse's. More than one spouse can claim retirement benefits; your former spouse's remarriage will not affect this right.

With some 205 million Social Security accounts, there are bound to be mistakes. To ensure that you are receiving credit for the income you have earned, periodically check that your earnings are being correctly reported. To check your account, request a statement of earnings (form SSA7004) from your local Social Security office or from the Commissioner of Social Security, 6410 Security Boulevard, Baltimore, Maryland, 21235. A few weeks after you return the completed form, you should receive a review of your work life and earnings as recorded by the Social Security Administration. A 24-hour toll-free hotline can shortcut the process (1-800-772-1213).

FREEBIE

Female readers would be interested in a free guide called *Social Security: What Every Woman Should Know*. It covers employment taxes, changes in marital status, and retirement. Write: Consumer Information Center, #526B, Pueblo, CO 81009.

Benefits are always under review. For example, budget discussions frequently look at the possibility of reducing cost-of-living allowances and shifting the age at which payment commences. In addition, the 1983 reforms in the Social Security system provided that for retirees born after 1938, the retirement age will be increased by two months for each year up to the new maximum benefit retirement age of 67 for those born after 1960. Early retirement at age 62 will still be an option, but the benefit will be decreased to 70 percent of the maximum paid at age 67.

Under current law, if you reach age 65 in 1994 or later, you'll need to have been employed for 10 years or 40 quarters to collect your full retirement benefit. If you're 55 and haven't been contributing fully to the Social Security system (by deducting Social Security taxes from your paycheck), you should make a point of doing so even if you must pay additional self-employment tax. To keep this part of your retirement solid, keep abreast of the changes in retirement rules such as selecting the age at which you will retire. In so doing, you'll receive full benefit from this pillar of your retirement plan.

THE SECOND PILLAR: HOME OWNERSHIP OR RENT REPLACEMENT

For future security and growth, purchasing property is the most significant investment you can make. Real estate outperforms other investments. Residential real estate provides the classic trade-off between tax shelter and growth. The interest is by and large deductible as are property taxes. As for capital gains, with a residence, you can roll over or defer paying tax on the profits as long as you buy a new home of equal or greater value within two years of the sale of your original home.

As a key part of retirement planning, a secure living space is critical (see "Steps to Home Ownership" in Chapter 7). But not all of us will be able to afford to buy our own homes. If you have been permanently priced out of the housing market, it's critical that you take active steps to ensure you can afford to be a renter by retirement time.

You'll need to set aside enough to cover your rent today plus inflation, assuming you'd want to continue at your current lifestyle level. Although there isn't an exact correlation between rents and inflation, rents, in general, rise parallel to the inflation rate. To figure the amount of rent money you would need in the future, you would have to estimate the affect of inflation.

Inflation levels cannot be predicted with certainty. Over the last decade inflation rose by 84 percent. Assuming the past decade is a reasonable guide, if your rent in 1990 is $1,000, by the year 2000, the equivalent rent would be $1,840, and by 2010, $3,680. Among your investments, savings, pensions, and Social Security, you have to conserve enough resources to pay your future inflation-adjusted rent—a "home-replacement fund."

With these numbers, such a task can seem overwhelming. A key strategy is to put your home-replacement fund in investments that have growth potential, so they, too, will rise with inflation and keep pace with rising rents.

Figuring zero inflation, for $12,000 rent a year (or $1,000 a month) at 10 percent interest (that's high), you would need a fund of $120,000 on top of all other living expenses to defray your annual rent of $12,000. If the home-replacement fund is in an equity-growth investment, you could figure on this target amount. To reach a fund of $120,000, you need to set aside $12,000 a year to retire in 10 years (not counting compounding interest).

Depending on your age, the number of years to retirement, and your expectations about retirement lifestyle, you need to add a target for rent replacement to your current financial goals. Obviously, if retirement is years off, this component can be a small amount. But if retirement is near, you must make this an absolute priority. Reaching this level of savings will obviously be impossible for many single parents. The alternative is to live in reduced circumstances for an unknown number of retirement years or to purchase property.

If necessary, sacrifice savings to buy a home. Even though you may violate the recommended savings level of three months of income, if you can get into a home of your own, in almost all cases, you should buy the house.

Once you have the funds for a down payment, you'll watch your equity grow as you pay off your mortgage and approach retirement. But again, if you can't purchase, engage in the rent-replacement strategy.

THE THIRD PILLAR: AN IRA, PENSION, OR OTHER RETIREMENT FUND

If you qualify for a company pension with sufficient vested benefits (meaning you'll receive the funds even if you change jobs, usually after a minimum of five years), then you have this base covered. If you can possibly afford it, add to your coverage by investing in IRAs or contributing to a 401(k) plan. Following are specifics about each type of fund.

For Everyone: Individual Retirement Accounts (IRAs) and Annuities

IRAs, or Individual Retirement Accounts, allow you to set aside funds for retirement while permitting you to defer taxes on the initial contribution of up to $2,000 annually as well as the interest income. Currently, you can qualify for tax deferment if you are not actively involved in a company pension or even with a pension, if your taxable income is below $25,000 and you're single. The maximum IRA contribution is $2,000 annually for an individual earner and is reduced on a sliding scale up to an adjusted gross income of $35,000 for single-income earners or heads of household. Even if you don't qualify for deferral on the contributions, the ability to earn tax deferred interest makes it a worthwhile investment.

IRA accounts can range from interest-only savings accounts (lower risk), to equity-based investments like mutual funds and stocks (higher risk), but no matter what your investment choice, an IRA grows much more quickly than monies put away with after-tax funds because of the tax-shelter feature. If you invest the same amount of money in an IRA for 30 years that you put in a nontax-advantaged account, for the 15 percent bracket, you'll gain almost $100,000 more in the IRA, of course the gains increase with the higher tax brackets. Putting your IRA money in mutual funds is a good way to start investing if you're an inexperienced investor. However, make sure you understand the type of funds you choose and their levels of risk. For example, equity funds fluctuate as the stock market fluctuates.

Withdrawals from IRAs must begin by age 70½, and a penalty fee is charged for withdrawal before age 59½. You can take money out of the account and pay a penalty if funds are needed early for an emergency.

If you're considering investing in an IRA but are afraid early withdrawal penalties will outweigh gains, consider that there is a crossover point at which you can actually come out ahead even with the penalty. Because the crossover point depends on interest rates, if you earn eight percent interest on your monies in the IRA the first year and must make an early withdrawal with a penalty of 10 percent, you will lose two percent. But after two years, you will have made 16 percent on the capital, not compounded, and with a 10 percent penalty for early withdrawal, you will have crossed over into a gain of six percent.

It is possible to avoid the 10 percent early withdrawal penalty if you annuitize your withdrawals over a period of time rather than taking them in one lump sum. A formula based on your life expectancy is used to figure the amount of your withdrawals and you must continue making the withdrawals for five years or until age 59½, whichever is later.

Remember, however, that taxes must be paid on the withdrawn sum according to your bracket. For example, a $2,000 withdrawal the second year would incur a 10 percent penalty of $200 plus $560 in taxes if you are in the 28 percent tax bracket. So you pay $760 to withdraw $2,000, leaving you with $1,240 cash and the balance in the account to continue to accrue tax-deferred interest. However, you would have had the use of the money tax-free for two years.

If you have a minimum of $2,500, you may want to consider an **annuity** as an additional supplement to your retirement funds. An annuity is a contract bought from an insurance company, and the holder pays a set sum of money. This money (plus interest) is then paid back at a predetermined date for either a set period of time or for the life of the contract holder.

You can cash in an annuity at any time, although there's a penalty for early withdrawal. The smallest annuity available is usually $2,500. The insurance company will apply charges that include a sales fee. You receive a tax break with a *deferred* annuity because the interest accrues with taxes deferred until withdrawal at retirement. This option is a good supplementary retirement plan.

If You Work for Someone Else: Qualified Retirement Plans

Qualified retirement plans sponsored by the employer come in two basic varieties: *Defined-benefit* and *defined-contribution*. Defined-benefits pension programs, in which the employer promises to pay the employee a specified amount per year at retirement, are no longer the norm.

More popular now are *defined-contribution* plans, which set the size of the employer and/or employee contributions and pay out whatever yield the investment has accrued. They allow the employer to make tax deductible contributions while the employee contributes pre-tax dollars. 401(k)s are a common variety of defined-contribution plans.

A portion of your defined-benefit pension may be insured by the Pension Benefit Guarantee Corporation even if the company goes bankrupt. However, if you participate in a *self-directed* program such as a 401(k), you are responsible for the investment decisions, and your employer is not required to insure it. If your job includes retirement benefits, take time to learn the details of your particular fund.

The major benefit of a pension plan—apart from the retirement security it provides—is the income tax shelter it provides for both the employer and the employee. The employer's contributions are deductible, and the employees defer tax payment on pension income until the monies are received. Thus, an individual may well choose to take a lower-paying position that offers a higher pension benefit.

Two points particularly concern single parents. Federal law requires that pensions must vest (be converted to your ownership) over a maximum of 6-7 years, depending on the plan. This provision is meant to protect those whose work lives involve interruptions.

Second, upon divorce, some pension benefits may still be yours. Unless you waive your right at divorce, federal law entitles you to a minimum of 50 percent of the accrued vested benefit in your spouse's plan. Technically, it is considered a survivor's benefit. If you are going through a divorce, have your attorney draft a QDRO (Qualified Domestic Relations Order, pronounced "quadro") which will direct the retirement plan administrator as to what payments are to be made to the divorced spouse.

As a supplement or an alternative to the company pension, consider a 401(k) plan (named after the section of the IRS code that defines it) if your company offers one. These *salary-reduction* plans involve employees' voluntarily diverting pretax salary to retirement or other employee benefit programs. Salary reduction is an excellent solution if you will not be with an employer long enough to qualify for full regular pension benefits from the company plan.

The largest number of new plans currently offered are 401(k) plans. In fact, because contributions are withdrawn before employers see the money, median income workers are twice as likely to participate in 401(k)s as to fund an IRA.

People employed by IRS code 501(c)(3) organizations—public school systems and certain nonprofit educational, charitable, literary, scientific, or religious organizations—are eligible for a similar salary-reduction plan under IRS code 403(b). The plan for nonprofit employees offers tax benefits similar to those in the 401(k). In addition, the employer has the option to contribute an additional amount in the employee's name to increase the employee's retirement benefit.

Both salary-reduction plans offer tax benefits to the employer as well as to the employee. Your maximum reduction was originally $7,000, indexed for inflation annually. (In 1996, the indexed amount stood at $9,500. The IRS announces the indexed amount during each tax year—therefore, check annually for the current figure.)

Generally, if you participate in any qualified retirement plan you may not be able to make a deductible contribution to an IRA. Check with your accountant for the latest earnings test figure. If you can afford to do it, think in terms of funding your 401(k) to its maximum amount and then making a nondeductible contribution to an IRA if you still have extra funds to commit.

For the Self-Employed: Keoghs and SEP-IRAs

If you're self-employed and can afford to save more than the $2,000 upper limit on an IRA, take advantage of a Keogh plan. Or, you may consider a SEP-IRA in lieu of both.

A Keogh plan is a pension fund for any person who reports earnings from self-employment, regardless of how small. Generally, there are three situations where you might encounter a Keogh—as an employee, as a self-employed person, or as partner or member of a board of directors.

If you're employed by someone else, your employer may contribute to your Keogh plan. If so, he or she is required by antidiscrimination laws to contribute the same percentage of your income to your Keogh as your employer contributes to his or her own Keogh. Usually, this contribution comes from the employer and not from your salary. If you're not self-employed, this is the only way a Keogh may apply to you.

If, however, you are the sole proprietor of a business, you may set up a Keogh for yourself. There are two basis types of Keogh plans: *defined-contribution* plans and *defined-benefit* plans. With defined-contribution plans (a discussion follows), you contribute a certain amount of your income, which is fixed by law. On the other hand, a defined-benefit plan allows annual payments according to your predetermined retirement income needs. This plan works best if you have ample discretionary funds and are fairly close to retirement.

Defined-contribution plans are the most common types of Keoghs. They offer two options, depending on your payment plan. If you fix an annual percentage of income to be contributed when you first open the account, you may contribute up to 20 percent of your earned income with a $30,000 maximum. However, if you want to have the option of paying differing percentages each year, you may contribute up to 13 percent of your earned income.

Partners and members of boards of directors (and self-employed people who employ others) may also open Keoghs. However, remember, if you employ others, you must match percentages with their salaries, potentially making a Keogh very expensive.

With Keogh plans, no matter what type, you determine whether the funds will be released in a lump sum or in installments. You also decide how you want the funds invested—in a money market, variable universal life insurance policy, an interest-bearing bank account, or any combination of these. However, you do have certain limitations with your Keogh such as those on IRAs. For instance, you are generally not allowed to withdraw money without a penalty until age 59½ or until you become disabled. And you must begin withdrawing money from your Keogh plan when you reach age 70½ even if you haven't retired.

The calculations in Keoghs are complex, so it's a good idea to seek professional advice if you're considering this plan.

Another option is the **Simplified Employee Pension, or SEP-IRA**. Like regular IRAs, SEP-IRAs offer tax sheltered contributions and interest income. The maximum yearly contribution is up to 15 percent of your gross income, not to exceed $22,500 in one year. The simplified paperwork required often makes it a good choice for self-employed persons who do not have any other employees and are not concerned about being able to take loans out against their funds.

But the SEP-IRA is not for everyone. If your small business offers any other type of pension benefits you may not use a SEP-IRA. In addition, if you use a SEP-IRA you must offer the same benefits to your qualifying employees as you offer yourself. Qualifying employees are those to whom you've paid at least $400 in a given year and have worked three out of the previous five years, so depending on your circumstances, you might be required to cover a lot of people. Stuart Raffel, President of Price, Raffel, & Browne Administrators, Inc. points out that many have gotten in hot water by choosing SEP-IRAs without consulting professional advice because the initial paperwork (IRS Form 5305A SEP) appears so simple.

RETIREMENT PLANNING CHECKLIST

☑ Estimate your approximate living expenses for retirement (about 70 percent of your pre-retirement income).

☑ Make sure you are adequately covered by disability and health insurance, including long-term care (see Chapter 11). Find out what role Medicare will play in your medical future and how to supplement with Medigap policies.

☑ List all benefits that you already have coming, such as Social Security, pensions through work, or plans you've set up for yourself such as IRAs.

☑ Make informed choices about supplemental retirement vehicles. If you must change jobs and you have a vested pension, roll it over into a roll-over IRA to continue the tax shelter benefits.

☑ Learn to manage your retirement investments according to your stage in life. When you are younger, for example, you can afford to invest in stocks which have a higher return overall but may also drop. Your younger age gives you time to ride out the low points. As you near retirement age you will be shifting more of your investments into more stable vehicles such as CDs.

☑ Plan to buy a home or provide enough income for rent.

RESOURCES

AARP (American Association of Retired Persons) 1909 K Street, N.W., Washington, DC 20049.

The Bronfenbrenner Life Course Center at Cornell University, 607-255-5557.

Karen Ferguson and Kate Blackwell. *The Pension Book: What You Need to Know to Prepare for Retirement.* New York: Arcade, 1995.

The National Center for Retirement Research, 1-800-426-7386.

Where to Look for Help with a Pension Problem. Available for $8.50 from The Pension Rights Center, 918 16th Street NW, Suite 704, Washington, DC 20006-2902.

CHAPTER 14

Where There's a Will

A will is especially important for single parents who must name a guardian for their children as well as make sure they inherit. If they're underage, you'll want to provide a trust or otherwise protect their financial interests in your will.

Sixty percent of all estates in America transfer through the intestacy laws.

Dying without a will or a will substitute such as a revocable living trust is an invitation for the state to choose your heirs for you. In fact, if your divorce isn't complete, your ex could end up your heir.

A durable power of attorney is also important to ensure that someone is designated to sign checks and make other financial decisions if you're incapacitated. With no spouse for "backup," you can't afford to overlook this second critical document—otherwise, who would pay the rent or buy the groceries if you were hit by a truck and in a coma?

PREPARING A LEGALLY BINDING ESTATE PLAN

If you don't prepare a legally binding estate plan with a will and a trust, state intestacy laws will designate your heirs and the dispersal of your property. Failure to consult an appropriate advisor can cause critical problems when legal loopholes or ill-chosen wording in your document make a mockery of your true wishes.

Self-help can be dangerous when so much is at stake. Instead, use your self-help kits or books to educate yourself, then seek counsel to ensure that your measures were appropriate. At the very least, dying intestate (without a legally binding estate plan) can be burdensome to your relatives and children. At worst, the consequences can be devastating.

State Intestacy Laws

Whether you fail to make a will or make one early on and don't update it, the state will step in to disburse your property, choose a guardian for your children, and select an administrator. Since laws vary by state, you would need to check your own state's intestacy laws to determine how you would be specifically affected. But why not use that same energy to begin your estate planning? If you don't, the following consequences may apply:

In general, spouses receive one-third to one-half the estate and *issue*, or your children (which may or may not include adopted children), receive the rest of the estate to be divided among them. This type of provision could be a problem for single parents whose divorces have not been finalized.

If you prepare a will but then remarry, your spouse will get the intestate share, in community property states, or what is known as a *forced* or *elective share*, which may be smaller than the intestate share, in common law states. To provide for your new spouse and your children, you should revise your will or draft a new one when you remarry.

Likewise, *pretermitted heir statutes* in most states are predicated on the idea that failure to mention a child in a will was an oversight, so the omitted child should get a share of the estate.

State intestacy laws don't provide for charitable gifts, so if you wanted to leave a gift to your college or favorite charity, you're out of luck.

The Importance of Advisors

While it is pertinent to engage in a certain amount of self-help to build your knowledge, your self-help should not replace the service of a reputable lawyer or accountant. Even official-looking will forms, kits, or computer programs should be approached cautiously.

Any but the simplest asset base and family structure will require both an attorney and an accountant. As a single parent, your family structure is probably too complex to attempt estate planning on your own especially if you have had multiple marriages or if the children in your custody have different biological parents than their siblings. In addition, if

A HEARTBEAT AWAY

For single parents, estate planning usually has one key goal: to protect your children, especially minors, in the case of your death. Thinking your children are one heartbeat away from being orphans—the melodramatic view of the situation—makes it all the more burdensome to tackle this fearsome topic alone.

The simplest way to begin estate planning is to determine the answers to a few questions. Your answers will help determine what types of legal documents you should use to secure your final wishes regarding your estate.

1. Do you have real property, such as a home, land, and so on?

2. Do you have an estate over the legally maximum amount that can be inherited tax free? (Currently $600,000—tax law revisions may be forthcoming.)

3. Do you have other property, besides real property, that requires special treatment?

4. Do you have a legal and financial guardian selected for your children?

Your task in estate planning is to determine the answers to these questions, for they, in turn, will help determine the sort of estate plan you need. Use the answers to the questions above to help you with the items below.

1. List your assets.

2. Estimate total value.

3. Decide on your heirs.

4. Pick a financial guardian for your children.

5. Pick a guardian of your child's person.

6. Choose an estate executor different from the guardian.

you have adopted, ancient rules regarding "bloodlines" that underlie some states' legal provisions could stand in the way of your child's rightful inheritance.

While insurance death benefits may be a large part of your estate planning if your assets are limited, you shouldn't trust insurance agents posing as financial planners to put together your estate plan. Those with larger estates must realize that handling the planning yourself may cost your heirs more in legal fees and taxes later on.

After your concerns about heirs and property are considered, federal tax laws will come into play to help you determine how to set up your actual estate. Your lawyer or accountant should inform you about how local estate, death, or inheritance taxes would affect your estate. Generally, the larger the estate, the more these state variances will matter. If you have assets located abroad, you will need to consult a specialist to deal with international tax issues that apply.

A WILL, A TRUST, OR BOTH?

While a will states how your money or property will be dispersed among your heirs, trusts tie certain monies to specific uses. Trusts give you a way to keep control of your assets even after passing away. In other words, you can't take it with you, but you can still have some control over how it's used.

If, like most people, your taxable estate is under $600,000, no special tax concerns govern your choice of documents. If your concern is mainly to see that your money passes hassle-free to your immediate family (i.e., children), you can employ a living trust in combination with a will. The will would cover residual gifts (for property left outside of the trust) and guardianship appointments.

At the opposite extreme are the super wealthy, who pay estate taxes at rates of up to 55 percent on their estate. To minimize the impact of these taxes, a variety of tax moves are required. These estate plans will also usually be carefully designed to meet additional objectives, such as preserving wealth for several family generations and making significant donations to charity. The bigger the estate, the more complex the objectives are likely to be, prompted in part by tax avoidance and in part by the desire to leave a mark on the world. These folks should consult more advanced estate planning literature, such as *Managing Your Inheritance*.

Your age may be a factor since the younger you are, the more likely a simple, less expensive will should suffice. A will avoids the hassles involved in transferring title each time assets change as the young adult progresses through life. However, if the same young single parent owned a condominium, a living trust would allow it to pass directly to children without probate costs or delays.

Another variable affecting the choice is whether there's a business involved. A young businesswoman with a business partner would have to think twice about a living trust, because placing the business assets in the trust could involve additional paperwork for every transaction, which could inhibit both business dealings and credit opportunities. For her, a will would work best.

Within the past few years, trusts have gained popularity as a way to circumvent lengthy probate codes and save on estate taxes and legal fees. Do-it-yourself kits abound and many consumers are confused. Aren't trusts for wealthy people? Do they replace my will or complement it? Do I need a lawyer? Are trusts suitable for the estate planning needs of single parents? Here's a primer on the types and uses of various trusts:

Trusts

If provisions are not made to fund the trust, the legal document can become a moot point. In other words, somewhere there will be deeds, titles, or bank accounts designated to the trust. The document will name trustees (an individual or board of individuals) to control it and provisions on how to select replacements for them. While the variations and complexities of trusts are as individual as the desires and fears of the grantor, there are some basic types that each retain specific objectives and tax treatments.

Testamentary trusts, created by will at the death of the grantor, cannot be modified except by the express modification provisions, if any, contained in the will.

Inter vivos trusts, set up to take effect during the life of the trust grantor, include both *revocable living trusts* and *irrevocable trusts.*

Revocable living trusts can be modified or canceled so long as the grantor is alive. They are commonly used to avoid probate, for ease of administration, and for flexibility. They have no estate tax consequences. Adults who don't have a relative or close friend should set up a revocable living trust and name a bank as the trustee.

Once created, **irrevocable trusts** cannot be changed, except within some limited parameters that must be outlined in the original trust document. They can be used to shelter assets from estate taxes in a number of ways. For example, up to $1 million can pass to grandchildren (or to anyone two generations down from the grantor).

If you're planning to remarry, you should be aware that *marital deduction trusts* allow you to pass an unlimited amount tax-free to a spouse and up to $600,000 tax-free to later beneficiaries.

Wills

Some states are infamous for their lengthy and burdensome probate processes. Like one professor of law proclaimed, "never, never die in New York!" In such states, even the simplest of wills can be subjected to a lengthy run through the court systems.

However, there's a growing movement toward states' adopting Universal Probate Codes, or simplified probate codes that will streamline the systems and make laws that now vary dramatically from state to state more unified. If your state has adopted such a code, you'll probably be able to draft your will by hand (legally called a holographic will), with or without a witness. While a hand-drafted will is better than nothing, it's always safest to draft a formal, witnessed, and lawyer-approved will.

Wills are about more than money and taxes; they also provide protection for your minor children. Your children and dependent parents require special thought.

Children often think much more about their parents' death than parents realize, so it is essential both to make plans and to communicate them to your children.

Also, be sure to discuss guardianship plans fully with any potential guardians as well as with your children. Don't appoint someone as a guardian unless they expressly agree. Then to be sure your wishes are followed, include the details in your will or living trust document.

If you're divorced, you'll need to reach agreement on the choice of guardian with former spouse, and both your individual wills should reflect this agreement. The physical guardian of your children, for example, your sister, needn't be the same as the legal or financial guardian, for example, your attorney. In fact, if necessary, you can provide all three. You might have a loving sister that would make a good parent, a family lawyer who would serve as the best overall custodian of legal questions that might arise, and a financially capable friend whom you would trust to protect your child's financial future by ensuring that your assets were kept intact for your child or children.

Take time to sit with your children and discuss your plans. Express that while you expect to be around for a long time, the reality is that no one knows exactly how long his or her life will be. If possible, empower your children by allowing them to assist in the arrangements you make, especially for physical custody.

If you're a single parent with a living former spouse who is the natural or adoptive parent of your children, the law generally assumes that the other parent will become the children's guardian. If you have concerns that the finances would not be properly handled, you can still separate the financial arrangements and appoint a trustee for the money in your estate, leaving your former spouse with only physical custody. In marriages where money was an issue, this plan will provide you peace of mind regarding your children's future welfare.

Failing to appoint a guardian can lead to protracted and costly litigation with various relatives and even friends laying claim to parenting your children. While possibly motivated by the best of intentions, the effect on the children can be devastating.

The same set of concerns holds true if you have aging parents who count on you for all or part of their support. In this instance, you might wish to leave the money in trust for them or arrange for a financial custodian to provide for them and preserve the funds.

If you have adopted children, be sure to specifically include them in the language of your will. Because of antiquated rules that trace back bloodlines for the purpose of selecting kings and earls, our own laws sometimes omit adopted children.

In one case, a childless beneficiary of a trust adopted a child. Because of the trust language chosen ("issue of my body" rather than "natural and adopted children"), the remainder of the trust would not go to the adopted child but to a distant cousin. Be sure to protect your own adopted children. Nothing could be more devastating to these children than to learn that, after all, they are not full family members.

If you fear that the other parent will somehow disinherit your child, you should realize that sanctity of family is sufficiently strong that the law looks with disfavor on such practices. Between generations, the reasonable expectation exists that family money, property, and personal mementos will be passed from one generation to the next. The law assumes that children will inherit equally from their parents.

Disinheritance is more common for adult children who have disappointed their parents. There is also a growing trend toward the wealthy giving only modest inheritances to their children out of a belief that they should learn to make their own way.

As discussed in Chapter 2, your marital dissolution agreement should include a clause that prohibits your former spouse from neglecting your child in favor of a new family. If there was never a marriage but paternity was established and child support paid, you should ask your lawyer whether there are estate planning issues from the other parent's perspective and how much control you have over them.

Much of estate planning advice centers on married couples. Estate tax law provides huge breaks for married persons. No such similar provisions occur with single persons or people who have chosen to live together without marrying. But the new social reality is that many unmarried couples want to ensure that their relationships are preserved in their estate plans because no spousal exemption is available.

Putting property in both names or in a living trust can protect this commitment. Either joint tenancy or a living trust can protect the surviving partner. However, property passed through joint tenancy or placed in a revocable trust is still considered part of the gross estate for tax purposes, so estate taxes cannot be avoided through this arrangement if the estate of either partner exceeds $600,000.

Also, in the case of unmarried persons who have children together, these children are legally "illegitimate." In some states, their rights to their parents' property are, nevertheless, recognized (with the best protection in Louisiana). However, by preparing a will or trust that makes intentions clear, such children can be best protected.

With homosexual couples, additional problems of inheritance can occur if the couple suffers family disapproval. If one partner's inheritance comes from ancestors, the family may feel it has a stake in the disposition of "family" money.

Some states permit adult adoption between homosexual couples. After an official adoption, the couple can gain some of the estate planning protections offered other legally recognized family members, such as an intestate share if the deceased partner's will is found invalid.

OTHER VITAL CONSIDERATIONS

Some of the most important aspects of estate planning for single parents are not necessarily covered in your will or trust documents. Related and vital tasks you must complete include designating an individual with *durable powers of attorney* privileges, making your medical wishes known in a *living will,* and easing the burden on your friends and family in their time of grief with *burial instructions and arrangements.*

Durable Powers of Attorney

The durable power of attorney allows your loved ones or attorney to carry on for you when you are not in a position to help yourself. Whereas the living will deals with preserving or letting go of your physical self, the durable power of attorney deals with the mental and physical capacity to cope with your financial and legal affairs.

Properly drawn, the durable power allows others to take over for you when you are temporarily or permanently incapacitated. Unlike *conservatorship,* which requires a court order for someone to step in and help you, the durable power of attorney has flexibility.

The durable power of attorney for health care (DPCH) enables you to delegate to anyone the power to make decisions about your medical treatment during your incapacity, including the decision to terminate life support. Because of the complexity of the legal, ethical, and medical issues involved in this area, it is important that your DPHC be made in strict accordance with your local laws. Medical professionals are usually willing to work with attorneys-in-fact, but want to protect against potential litigation in this highly charged area.

This power can be set up as either a separate document if your estate plan includes a will or as a part of your living trust document if you have a family trust, and it is governed by state law.

ALL THE RIGHT PLACES: WHERE TO KEEP VITAL DOCUMENTS

Details such as where to put each estate planning document can be critical, but sometimes professionals stop short of providing this all-important advice.

Will: You should have only one original will, but keep copies of your will in at least three locations: with your attorney, in your safety deposit box, and with a close relative or at your home. Opening a safety deposit box involves legal steps that may consume valuable time if your executor and others are not aware of your wishes.

Living Trust: This document should be kept in the same locations as the will. You will also have deeds for property belonging to the trust that should be kept with the original trust document.

Living Wills: Put this document on file at your family or primary care physician's office as well as the family attorney. Place another copy with other key documents and keep them together in a marked envelope in your home. Share a copy of this document with close family members and verbally reinforce your wishes.

Durable Power of Attorney: An original of this document should be on file with your family attorney as well as with a key family member or the person who would exercise the power.

Burial Instructions: Since they will be needed immediately, leave your burial instructions somewhere that can be readily accessible to your survivors. Include information about the location of your will with these instructions. Locate a copy in your home and place backup copies with your minister or rabbi, a trusted friend, and even your doctor. A master copy should also be left with your attorney and in your safety deposit box. But remember, either a death certificate or a court order is ordinarily required to open the safety deposit box even if you have made an heir a signatory, because such boxes are frozen upon the death of the box renter.

Living Wills

Some states allow a living will that directs your doctors regarding the extension of your life by extraordinary measures. This enables you to leave clear written information on your views about preserving your own life in the face of lingering illness. Like the DPHC, the living will must strictly comply with state law. Unlike the DPHC, the living will can be used only by your physicians in extremely limited circumstances.

Be sure to indicate your wishes about artificial life support for extended periods, organ donations, and autopsies. Be as explicit as you can. These decisions often involve hefty hospital fees, so your loved ones could find themselves facing a "my money for your life" choice. Under life and death pressure, few of us would say of a loved one, "don't spend the money." Your guidance, planned in advance, will help your significant others tremendously.

Burial Instructions and Arrangements

Because the funeral industry has come under serious criticism in recent years, the Federal Trade Commission (FTC) has promulgated regulations that attempt to protect unwary and vulnerable consumers. However, rather than rely on arms-length federal assistance, provide your heirs with clear instructions about your own preferences.

Know the burial costs and customs of your area, but don't assume that you'll die where you live now. Many funeral homes offer a "preneed funeral arrangement" linked to the services of their particular establishments. If a person dies in a different location from the funeral home, these policies are often not worth their price because the cost of flying the body back might exceed the cost of the burial.

In planning your own funeral, remember to specify the following items:

1. The type of service you want.

2. The type of burial or cremation.

3. If burial, the type and general expense level of the casket.

4. The location where you wish to be buried.

5. Any other information that's important to you.

Obviously, to think these issues through, you'll need to do some research. If getting caught up in plot purchasing turns you off—and why not?—then talk with your extended family. If you're an urban resident in a major city, plots can be prohibitively expensive, and if bought under burial pressure, difficult to choose. Better: See if members of your family are buried in locations outside the city where a grave can be added. The cost of flying a body and casket runs about the same as a coach fare, so this solution may be preferable to some than the cost of an urban plot.

Although it's easy to ignore issues such as whether you have burial insurance and where you would wish to be buried, single parents must make these decisions, so the burden does not fall on others. It's not easy to contemplate one's own death in such detail; however, the alternative is to leave the chore for others to deal with at a most difficult time.

RESOURCES

Emily Card and Adam Miller. *Managing Your Inheritance.* New York: Random House, 1997 (forthcoming).

Winifred Conkling. *Securing Your Child's Future: A Financial and Legal Guide for Parents.* New York: Random House, 1995.

Conclusion

Throughout this book, the fact that you might have a significant other or potential life partner lined up has been purposely ignored. As emphasized before, your finances don't occur in a vacuum. Neither does your status as a single parent. Since one of the only constants in life is what we can do for ourselves, the focus of this book is truly on "self-help" to empower you as a single parent.

CONSIDERING REMARRIAGE

However, statistics suggest that you may become romantically involved again. In fact, the U.S. Department of the Census estimates that the number of divorced women projected to remarry eventually to about two-thirds. Past figures were higher—about three-fourths of divorced women remarried. Believe it or not, no government statistics are kept on the remarriage rate of men!

Of those that remarry, four out of ten of those (and all) marriages will end in divorce, down from the half of the 1970s and 1980s.

Statistics won't tell us whether you'll remarry, but the chances are you've at least thought about it. Before considering marriage again, if you are a divorced single parent, learn from the past and incorporate those lessons into your future plans.

> **"Remarriages are a triumph of hope over experience."**
> —Oscar Wilde

Also, if you do remarry, you are starting later in life with more pre-exisiting financial and familial obligations. Don't take a single step towards making binding legal ties without looking at the material in Appendix 5.

At the bottom line, your romantic alignments are also legal and financial ones. Act accordingly and seek financial and legal advice right alongside the premarital counseling.

Not the Remarrying Kind

While marriage looks great as the evenings grow cooler and the nights shorter around the holidays, at a Christmas dinner with two close friends, I realized just how many changes would be involved for me to remarry. This point was driven home to me one night at dinner.

George and Sharon are one of the happiest couples I know, having raised two wonderful children. They are now able to luxuriate in many of life's pleasures, including an occasional meal at the finest restaurants. But with spread-out Los Angeles lifestyles, they arrived at dinner in two separate cars to avoid going home during rush hour. After a lovely meal, their casual discussion over the proper route home (more than 45 minutes away) turned into a heated debate.

She wanted to go her familiar route and, for safety, he wanted her to take his favorite way while he followed close behind. I may never know how it was settled, but I enjoyed the relative peace of my solo drive home on the route I chose with no contention. Yes, for some of us there are distinct benefits to being single. For now, I have found my way and I am happy with it.

Don't feel compelled to marry again if you have found a center for yourself as an individual. One day things may change again, but try to enjoy each stage of life as it comes along, even your solitude.

Putting Your Experience to Work

Sometimes the complications of daily living make it hard for us to find energy to give to others. Yet, as a single parent, you are part of an important political constituency whose voice is often silent. Recently a *Los Angeles Times* article pointed out that for the first time in history, women members of Congress can bring their special voices to bear on the Congressional process. In the past, when Representatives were mostly men, women's everyday experiences simply weren't part of the legislative fabric. But now, the Congress includes a former welfare mother, single parents of both sexes, and the second woman who has given birth while in Congress. All these life experiences have begun to find expression in the legislative chambers.

Likewise, your own particular experiences and concerns should be put to work to ensure a better life for you and others in your position. Women and men of both major political parties have looked at key legislative concerns that help improve the lives of single parents. You, too, should at least be aware of the following:

Family and Medical Leave Act, enacted in 1993, allows people in many job settings to keep their employment after family leave.

Violence Against Women Act, signed into law in 1995, to set up programs to curb domestic abuse.

Earned Income Tax Credit, of which women file 75 percent of claims, allows a tax refund paid in cash to working people whose incomes fall below the poverty line.

Reproductive Choice, a point of constant political contention, affects all of us when we turn to the issues of teen pregnancy, not to mention our own choices.

Minimum Wage increases: 58 percent of those who would benefit from an increase in the minimum wage are women, many supporting families.

TO WRITE TO CONGRESS

U.S. House of Representatives
Washington, D.C. 20515

U.S. Senate
Washington, D.C. 20510

Congressional Switchboard (202) 224-3121

THE PRESIDENT

The White House
1600 Pennsylvania Avenue, N.W.
Washington, DC 20500

White House Switchboard: (202) 456-1414

White House Fax: (202) 456-2641

If these issues are important to you, bring your special experience to bear on the political process. Let your Congressional representatives know your point of view and that it's based upon your own hard-won experience.

Staying Financially Independent

Don't try to do everything in this book. You can't fill out all the budget worksheets *and* plan cheap birthday parties *and* write the president all in one day! Getting your financial affairs in order is a lifelong process that begins with tiny steps. Take the first one today and place yourself on the road to security, solvency, and success. But remember, everyone's journey is unique. Don't lose sight of the day-to-day joys, and remember, money isn't everything.

APPENDIX 1

Accessing Government Financial Assistance

Eligibility is based on income, but working single parents may still meet the criteria. Call your state's Department of Health and Human Services for general information. The following programs are generally available:

1. **Women, Infants, and Children (WIC).** Pregnant or breastfeeding mothers and their infants and/or children must be deemed nutritionally at risk by their physicians to receive food vouchers (to be cashed in at participating grocery stores) through their local health department.

2. **Food Stamps.** Food stamps may be used to purchase food in participating grocery stores.

3. **Health care assistance.** Formerly known as Medicaid, now some individual states have adopted their own health care plans, such as TN-Care in Tennessee. Premiums are set on a sliding scale according to income.

4. **Commodities.** Government surplus items such as cheese, canned meat, flour, and cornmeal are distributed at specific locations and dates according to zip code. Participants must register ahead of time with the administering agency.

5. **Federal childcare assistance** helps single parents when they're at risk of losing a job because they can't afford the cost of daycare. The federal subsidy for private daycare

costs typically lasts 1–2 years and can provide a buffer zone for those leaving AFDC as well.

6. **Job rehabilitation.** Some job training programs are targeted to disabled citizens. Others are linked with welfare reform—giving AFDC recipients a chance to strike out on their own.

7. **Aid for Families With Dependent Children (AFDC).** AFDC provides small monthly checks to be used for living expenses.

APPENDIX 2

Helpful Organizations

CHILDCARE RESOURCES, INFORMATION, AND REFERRALS

Center for Parenting Studies
Weelock College 200
The Riverway
Boston, MA 02215
(617) 734-5200 ext. 214

Child Care Action Campaign
330 Seventh Avenue, 17th Floor
New York, NY 10001
(212) 239-0138

Child Care Aware
2116 Campus Drive, SE
Rochester, MN 55904
(800) 424-2246

Child Care Law Center
22 Second Street, 5th Floor
San Fransisco, CA 94105
(415) 495-5498

Children's Defense Fund
25 E Street, NW
Washington, DC 20001
(800) 233-1200

The Children's Foundation
725 Fifteenth Street, NW,
Suite 505
Washington, DC 20005

Families and Work Institute
330 7th Avenue, 14th Floor
New York, NY 10001
(212) 465-2044

International Child Resource
Institute
1810 Hopkins Street
Berkeley, CA 94707
(510) 644-1000

Lipton Corporate Child
Care Centers, Inc.
1233 20th Street, NW, Suite 701
Washington, DC 20036
(202) 416-6875

National Association of Child
Care Resource and Referral
Agencies (NACCRA)
1319 F Street, NW, Suite 608
Washington, DC 20004
(202) 393-5501

Call or write for information on
referrals in your area.

National Association for the
Education of Young Children
1509 Sixteenth Street, NW
Washington, DC 20036
(202) 424-2460

National Association for
Family Day Care
725 Fifteenth Street, NW,
Suite 505
Washington, DC 20005
(800) 359-3817

National Coalition to End
Racism in America's Child
Care System
22075 Koths
Taylor, MI 48180
(313) 295-0257

LEGAL AND FINANCIAL PLANNING

The American Academy
of Matrimonial Lawyers
150 North Michingan Avenue,
Suite 2040
Chicago, IL 60601
(312) 263-6477

American Association of Retired
Persons Social Outreach and
Support Section
601 E Street NW
Washington, DC 20049
(202) 434-2277

The Association for Children
for Enforcement of Support
2260 Upton Avenue
Toledo, OH 43606
(800) 537-7072

Center for Battered
Women's Legal Services
P.O. Box 3344
Church Street Station
New York, NY 10008
(212) 349-6009

Child Custody Evaluation
Services of Philadelphia
P.O. Box 202
Glenside, PA 19038
(215) 576-0177

Children's Defense Fund
25 E Street, N.W.
Washington, DC 20001
(202) 628-8787

Children's Rights Council
220 I Street, NE, Suite 140
Washington, DC 20002
(202) 547-6227

Clearinghouse on Pensions
and Divorce
Pension Rights Center
918 16th Street, NW Suite 704
Washington, DC 20006
(202) 296-3776

Committee for Mother
and Child Rights
210 Ole Orchard Drive
Clear Brook, VA 22624
(540) 722-3652

Consumer Product Safety
Commission
100 S. Wacker
Chicago, IL 60606
(312) 353-8260

Crittenton Services, Child
Welfare League of America
440 1st Street, NW, Suite 310
Washington, DC 20001
(202) 638-2952

Custody Action for Lesbian
Mothers
PO Box 281
Narberth, PA 19072
(610) 667-5760

Ex-Partners of Servicemen
for Equality (X-POSE)
P.O. Box 11191
Alexandria, VA 22312
(703) 941-5844

Find Dad
1440 N. Harbor Blvd., Suite 515
Fullerton, CA 92835
(800) 729-6667
This private collection agency
will retain a percentage of any
past due child support that they
collect on your behalf. If they fail
to collect, nothing is owed them.

Joint Custody Association
10606 Wilkins Avenue
Los Angeles, CA 90024
(310) 475-5352

National Center for Women
and Retirement Research
Long Island University
Southampton Campus
Southampton, NY 11968
(800) 426-7368

National Gay and Lesbian
Task Force
2320 17th Street, NW
Washington, DC 20009-2702
(202) 332-6483

NOW Legal Defense
and Education Fund
99 Hudson Street, 12th Floor
New York, NY 10013
(212) 925-6635

Pension Rights Center
918 16th Street, NW, Suite 704
Washington, DC 20006
(202) 296-3776

PARENTING RESOURCES

The Alliance for
Children's Rights
3600 Wilshire Boulevard,
Suite 1904
Los Angeles, CA 90010
(213) 368-6010

Big Brothers and Big Sisters
of America
230 North 13th Street
Philadelphia, PA 19107
(215) 567-7000

National Life Center
686 N. Broad Street
Woodbury, NJ 08096
(800) 848-LOVE

Children of Divorce
Education Program
P.O. Box 635
Carrolton, GA 30117
(404) 832-8964

The Children's Foundation
725 15th Street, NW, Suite 505
Washington, DC 20005
(202) 347-3300

Family Resources Coalition
236 N. Michigan Avenue,
Suite 1625
Chicago, IL 60601
(312) 341-0900

Family Service Association
of America
11700 West Lake Park Drive
Milwaukee, WI 53224
(414) 359-1040

National Center for Missing
and Exploited Children
2101 Wilson Boulevard,
Suite 550
Arlington, VA 22201
(800) 843-5678

Effectiveness Training
International
531 Stevens Avenue
Solana Beach, CA 92075
(619) 481-8121

Parents Without Partners
401 N. Michigan Avenue
Chicago, IL 60611-4267
(800) 637-7974

Single Mothers by Choice
P.O. Box 1642
Gracie Square Station
New York, NY 10028
(212) 988-0993

Single Parent Resource Center
31 East 28th Street, 2nd floor
New York, NY 10026
(212) 951-7030

Single Parents Association
4727 E Bell Road, Suite 45-209
Phoenix, AZ 85032
(602) 788-5511
(800) 704-2102 (outside of Arizona)
E-mail: spa@neta.com

Stepfamily Association
of America, Inc.
215 Centennial Mall S., Suite 212
Lincoln, NE 68508
(402) 477-STEP (402-477-7837)
(800) 735-0329

Stepfamily Foundation, Inc.
National Headquarters
333 West End Avenue
New York, NY 10023
(212) 877-3244

United Way, Community Services
Division
701 North Fairfax Street
Alexandria, VA 22314-2088
(703) 836-7100

YMCA National Headquarters
101 N. Wacker Drive, 14th Floor
Chicago, IL 60606
(312) 977-0031

Index

retirement and, 169–70
steps to, 98–100
Homeowner's insurance, 146–47,
147–48
Home-replacement fund, 169–70
Homework, children's, 16
Household maintenance, as
time-buster, 77–78
Housekeeper, hiring a, 81
Housing. *See also* Home
for college students, 164
Housing and Urban Development
hotline, 98
Housing discrimination, 98

I

Income
earning more versus spending time
with the kids, 67
increasing your, 66
of single mothers, 19
supplementing your, 70–74
Individual Retirement Accounts
(IRAs), 170–72
Infants, money and, 108
In-force policy ledger, 145
Installment purchase agreements,
103
Insurance, 139–52
automobile, 101, 146, 147
death of spouse and, 27
disability, 144–45
health, 19, 141–43
homeowner's, 146–47, 147–48
inventory of, 139–41
life, 19, 145–46
making claims, 150–52
for students, 113
Insurance agents, 148–49
Interest rates, mortgage, 99, 100

Internal Revenue Service, work-at-
home publications, 71
Internet, working at home and, 71
Interruptions from your children, 23
as time-buster, 76–77, 80
Inter vivos trusts, 182
Intestacy laws, state, 178, 179
Investing in yourself, 4
IRAs (Individual Retirement
Accounts), 166, 170–72
Irrevocable trusts, 183

J

Japanese, 49
Jinnett, Jerry, 71
Jobs, 163. *See also* Employment
finding, 68–69
part-time, 71–72
Job training programs, 195
Joint and several liability for tax
bills, 62

K

Kelly, Arabella, 47, 118
Keogh plans, 174–76
Kraehmer, Steffen T., 80

L

Landlords, 97
Large purchases, 102–4
Laundry, 96
Lawyers. *See* Attorneys
Lecturing, supplementing your
income by, 73
Letting go of the past (exercise),
31–32
Libraries, 83
Life insurance, 145–46